J. T. Mayne

**Short Notes of Tours in America and India**

J. T. Mayne

**Short Notes of Tours in America and India**

ISBN/EAN: 9783337241728

Printed in Europe, USA, Canada, Australia, Japan

Cover: Foto ©Andreas Hilbeck / pixelio.de

More available books at **www.hansebooks.com**

# SHORT NOTES

OF

# TOURS IN AMERICA AND INDIA.

BY

J. T. MAYNE,

ASSISTANT IN REVENUE BOARD OFFICE,
AND ORGANIST OF THE CATHEDRAL, MADRAS.

MADRAS:
GANTZ BROTHERS,
ADELPHI PRESS, 175, MOUNT ROAD.

1869.

# PREFACE.

Much that is contained in the following pages will, I fear, be considered a very old story, seeing that my tour in America was made in 1859, just ten years ago. The notes of that tour, which were compiled after my return to England, partly from notes and partly from actual letters, were thrown into the latter form entirely; as being on the whole the easiest style of writing for an inexperienced and "untrained" author. My little brochure would have seen the light (as much of it at least as is generally visible in London) nine years ago, had I been able to induce any one to publish it; which, as I may as well confess, I was not. The remembrance of this not very encouraging circumstance, together with the painful consciousness of the existence, in these letters, of a good deal of "twaddle" made me hesitate as to the expediency of publishing them now: but as I think some points are touched on, relating to matters ecclesiastical, which have been overlooked by most writers of "American notes," I venture to hope that some wheat may be extracted from the bundle of chaff, with which my readers are presented, and which I the less scruple to burden them with, in that "chaff" of another description will, I doubt not, overwhelm me for my presumption in thus rushing into print.

The notes of a tour in Bombay and Bengal were published originally in that much vilified print the "*Madras Churchman,*" and as several people were pleased to say, that the notes had interested them, and as my American letters by themselves would have made up a volume of utterly contemptible proportions, I have been induced to re-publish my slight experiences of the East along with those of the West.

J. T. M.

MADRAS, *January* 1869.

# CONTENTS.

## PART I.—LETTERS FROM AMERICA.

|  | Page. |
|---|---|
| LETTER I.—Description of the "Arabia" Steamship—The voyage | 1 |
| LETTER II.—Arrival at Halifax—The Harbour—Fort—Description of the City | 9 |
| LETTER III.—The Churches of Halifax — S. Paul's — S. George's — "Salem" Chapel — S. Luke's Cathedral — Roman Church—Style of services—Climate of Halifax | 17 |
| LETTER IV.—Departure from Halifax : Arrival at Boston—Hotel coaches and ferry steamers | 22 |
| LETTER V.—Hotels — Revere House — Street Railways — Cambridge — Harvard College—Chapel—Observatory—Christ Church—State House—Tremont Temple—Music Hall—Theatres—Dockyard—Bunker's Hill | 26 |
| LETTER VI.—Boston Churches : Church of the Advent—Trinity—S. Paul's — Stone Chapel — System of Fire alarms — Climate of Boston | 35 |
| LETTER VII.—Departure from Boston—American Railway—Steamer "Metropolis"—Arrival at New York | 39 |
| LETTER VIII.—General description of New York—Broadway—Fifth Avenue—Central Park—Theatres—Barnum's Museum—Hotels | 45 |
| LETTER IX.—The Shipping of New York—Ocean Steamers—The Collins and Cunard lines of Mail Steamers | 58 |
| LETTER X.—The Churches of New York : Trinity—S. Paul's—S. John's—Trinity Chapel—Grace Church—Calvary Church—S. Thomas'—Church of the Holy Innocents—Madison Street Mission—Church of the Holy Communion—Roman Churches—Unitarian Meeting House—Church feeling in New York—American Prayer Book—Church papers | 65 |
| LETTER XI.—American Society—Departure from New York—Hudson River—Railway journey between Albany and Niagara—Fire at Lockport—Arrival at Niagara—Sound of the Falls | 77 |
| LETTER XII.—Niagara—Description of the Falls—Moonlight visit to Goat Island—Visit to Brock's Monument and the Whirlpool—Buffalo—Roman Cathedral—Lake Erie—Steamer "Western Metropolis" | 85 |

LETTER XIII.—Departure from Niagara—Steamer on Lake Ontario—Kingston—River S. Lawrence—Lake of the Thousand Islands—Rapids of the S. Lawrence—Montreal—Roman Cathedral—New Anglican Cathedral—Festival of Corpus Christi—An ill spent Sunday afternoon—Convents—Departure from Montreal—Lake Champlain—Lake George—Fort William Henry—Charming specimen of an American Railway—Saratoga—Albany—Roman Cathedral and Church of S. Joseph—Return to Boston.................................................................................................... 93

LETTER XIV.—State of Organ building in America—Organs built by Erben of New York—Hook of Boston, and Simmons and Wilcox of Boston—Brooklyn—Trinity Church—American Oysters and Lager Beer...................................................................................... 106

LETTER XV.—Excitability of the New Yorkers—The Japanese Embassy "Sensation"—The "Great Eastern" Excitement—Arrival of the "Great Eastern"............................................................... 112

Journal kept on board the "Great Eastern"......................................... 117

## PART II.—NOTES OF A SHORT TOUR THROUGH THE NORTHERN PRESIDENCIES.

*Page.*

CHAPTER I.—Madras to Beypore—Voyage to Bombay—Bombay—Colaba Church—Cathedral. ............................................................. 133

CHAPTER II.—Bombay continued—Towers of Silence—Malabar Hill—Elephanta—Regatta in the Harbour—Bhore Ghaut............... 146

CHAPTER III.—Bombay to Nagpore—Church at Nagpore—Nagpore to Jubbulpore—Marble Rocks—Jubbulpore to Allahabad—Church at Allahabad..................................................................... 151

CHAPTER IV.—Delhi—Railway Station—Fort—Palace—Station Church—S. Stephen's Memorial Church............................................. 153

CHAPTER V.—Jumma Musjid—Kootub—Cashmere Gate—Arrival at Agra. 164

CHAPTER VI.—Agra—Fort—Taj—Akbar's Tomb—Cawnpore............... 160

CHAPTER VII.—Lucknow—Kaiser Bagh—Residency—Martiniere—Church—Benares—View from the River—College—Calcutta—Cathedral....................................................................... 174

CHAPTER VIII.—S. John's Church—Fort Church—S. James's Church.... 184

CHAPTER IX.—Bishop's College—Dum Dum—Climate of Calcutta, &c., —Return to Madras. ...................................................... 189

# LETTERS FROM AMERICA.

# LETTER I.

### On board the "Arabia,"
### *January* 1859.

THIS is the first day, since we fairly lost sight of Old England, that I have been able to collect my thoughts and writing materials, and to keep them sufficiently steady for a letter. Commend me to an Atlantic voyage in January, for an experience of the rise and progress of sea-sickness! But I know you would like me to "begin at the beginning," as I used to say in those long bye-gone days, when my greatest delight was in listening to the stories, original and otherwise, of which you had so large a store. I however have nothing to tell you at all resembling those old stories, but only some very matter-of-fact occurrences. It was a cold, foggy afternoon, when E. and I drove down to the landing-stage at Liverpool, accompanied by two friends, who were to see us safe on board the "Arabia" steam-ship, then at anchor in the Mersey, with her steam up, and ready for a start. On leaving the cab, we formed a small procession, in which my luggage took the lead, and with some difficulty made our way to a small red-funnelled steamer, moored at one corner of the landing-stage. About twenty of our future fellow-passengers were already on board the little vessel, most of them accompanied like ourselves by friends, determined to see the last of them. It was about as dreary a day, for leaving home, for the first time on an Atlantic voyage, as could well be imagined, and I thought, with a shudder, of the Nova Scotian winter that lay before us. Water and sky were all of one colour. At the wharf, alongside of which we were moored, the ferry steamers were bobbing up and down, under the influence of a very decided swell, which (together with the strong south-west wind then blowing) conjured up sundry frightful reminiscences of sea-sickness, not to be prevented from changing into equally frightful anticipations; even by the remembrance of the large stock of chloroform with which I was provided. Beyond the steamers, the forms of sundry vessels riding at anchor, could be indistinctly seen; whilst beyond them again, was an obscure something, which, by those acquainted with the locality, might have been recognized as Birkenhead. After a delay of about ten minutes, the lines were cast off, and we steamed out into the mist, in search of the "Arabia." I strained my eyes to the utmost, in vain endeavours to distinguish the vessel that was to be our home for the next fortnight; but at last gave up the attempt in despair, and wrapping my warm cloak more closely round me, sat down and turned my attention to other matters. I was roused by a sudden jerk; and on looking up, found our little steamer overshadowed by a huge round stern, with the red ensign flying on the staff, and the name "Arabia" printed above some sham stern-windows. We slowly glided up to the gangway, and soon our little party was safely transferred from the small ship to the large one. As you have never seen one of the justly-celebrated "Cunard Steamers," I think I may as well pause here and give you a description of our ship. As all these vessels are arranged in much the same way, to describe one, is to give a pretty fair idea of all. The "Arabia" is a ship of about 2,400 tons measurement, including her engine-room. She is 300 feet long over all, by 41 broad, and about 36 feet deep from the upper or spar-deck. She has two funnels, painted red with black tops; and two masts, both fully rigged with square sails. Her engines are of 1000 horse power, the paddle wheels being 36 feet in diameter.

So much for her external appearance. And now as regards her passenger arrangements. The upper deck of all may be called the promenade or spar-deck, and extends the entire length of the vessel, though not the whole width. It is, in fact, the roof of a long deck-house which occupies the greater portion of the main-deck—(save where interrupted by the crank hatches)—leaving a long narrow strip of the deck on each side, open to the air. This is so, however, only on the after-portion of the vessel, as, forward of the after-most funnel. The spar-deck extends the whole width of the ship, thus completely shutting in the main-deck. This arrangement, however, is peculiar to the "Arabia," the other vessels of the Company having the forward-part of the deck similar to the after-end. This spar-deck forms the favourite resort of the passengers in fine weather, but when the spray is flying too much to render the position pleasant, the narrow open strips of the main-deck on each side of the deck-house become the fashionable promenade. And now for the contents of this deck-house. At the extreme stern you have the steering chamber, with a raised roof with glass windows all round, so as to allow the steersman to see well forward on the spar-deck. There are generally only two wheels on the axle, though in bad weather I believe another one can be added. On each side of the steering chambers, are cabins for two of the officers. In front of these, comes the chief dining saloon. This is a handsome room about 70 feet long by 20 broad, and 8 feet high. It is fitted up in the ordinary way, and is well lighted by seven large windows on each side. Of course there is the usual quantity of mirrors and maplewood. Forward of this, and separated from it by a passage is the steward's pantry. This passage is indeed the entrance hall and has a door on each side opening from the main-deck. On each side of the saloon door is a well-filled book-case, and on each side of the pantry or bar-room door opposite, is a staircase leading down to the sleeping cabins, &c. on the lower deck. Continuing, however, our course forward, we pass in succession the captain's cabin and the kitchen. Here the deck-house ends, or rather seems to have split asunder, to make way for the crank hatches, as there are cabins on each side of the deck; at this point, for the use of the purser, baker, carpenter, &c., and last, though not least, the cow. Beyond the crank hatches, the deck-house joins itself together again in the centre of the vessel, and contains, in succession, the Engineer's cabin, the forward saloon, and lower deck staircase, and the seamen's berths, together with a number of other places which I cannot now enumerate. I forgot to mention that the entrance gangway is through the bulwarks of the main-deck, nearly opposite the saloon door, and close to it is the staircase leading up on to the spar-deck. The lower deck is occupied for its entire length (save where interrupted by the engine room) by a row of state rooms along each side. The entire centre space forward is also occupied by state rooms, and about fifty feet of the length aft, there being room in the remaining portion for two small saloons—one for gentlemen, the other for ladies. This latter is very prettily furnished, and the whole of the cabins are well ventilated, and have a height of 8 feet. Having thus endeavoured to give to you some idea of our ship, I will resume the narrative of my journey. My first move after seeing my luggage safely transferred from the tender to the "Arabia," was to rush into the saloon to secure a place at table. I might have spared myself the trouble. Only two tables, out of eight, were required for our small number, and had I foreseen the very slight acquaintance I was destined to form with the dinner table, I should have given myself no anxiety on the subject. As the time for departure drew near, our friends who were not to accompany us began to make their adieux, and the greater portion of them left in the steamer which brought us on board. *My* friends, however, determined to see the very last of us, obtained permission to land in the steamer which was to bring the mails. We accordingly sought the upper deck, and had been promenading up and down for some time deeply engaged in conversation, when thinking I felt some motion, I looked up, and lo! the long white wake astern shewed that we were positively off. The dismay of my friends may be imagined. They fully made up their minds to an unexpected Atlantic trip. To our great relief, however, we soon saw the little tender waiting for us; and as we passed her, she steamed up alongside, and without either vessel stopping, the mail-bags were brought on board, while my friends tumbled down the ladder into the tender, with more haste than ceremony. After seeing them safely down the perilous path, I ascended to the upper-deck and walked to the extreme stern in order to see the last, of what was now, the only link that bound us to the old country. Very soon the last mail-bag disappeared through the gangway, the lashings were cast off—a voice on the bridge gave the order, " Full speed," the little tender rapidly receded into the mist, through which I could just discern the white handkerchiefs of my friends waving their last adieux, and we were " off." It was now rapidly getting dark, and as the mist had already turned to rain, I hastened to take shelter in the saloon. Here dinner soon engaged our attention, and had I known how long it would be ere another good meal would fall to my lot, I think I should (if possible) have done it even greater justice than I did. You would be astonished, if you could see the dinners which they produce day after day on board these vessels—a bill of fare as long as my arm, and everything excellent. Dinner over, I took up a book and began to read. I tried hard to persuade myself, that the very unpleasant headache, which was forcing itself on my notice, was *not* the usual precursor of the dreaded sea-sickness. Did you ever watch any one undergoing the preparatory symptoms? It is a curious study, in more ways than one. You see the victim enter the cabin with a firm step and resolute eye. He seats himself on a sofa, (near the door) leaning well back, and holding a book in his hand. He smiles broadly at all the jokes, if there be any; but presently the book drops on the table; and the reader's head (leaning on one hand) is bent over it. By and bye the other hand is required to prop up the increasing weight—till at last (previously observing aloud for the benefit of those within hearing, that he is excessively fatigued) the unhappy man lies down at full length on the sofa; still however attempting to look unconcerned, and pretending to read the book which he yet retains. At this juncture he probably calls for a glass of brandy. If you have the heart to watch him further, you will perceive his eyes closing gradually; presently the book falls from his hand, and after a moment or two of ghastly quiet, he suddenly starts up, and makes a blind rush for the stairway. It generally happens that you don't see that individual again for some days. I did not remain in the saloon, beyond the first stage of the process, but retired in good season, with a serene countenance and a tranquil mind, for I thought of my chloroform, and was comforted. Deluded mortal! I found too late, alas, that there is no cure for seasickness; and I warn you to give no credit to any one, who tells you that there is. I took the prescribed dose, got into bed, and never was so ill in my life. I draw a veil over this part of my adventures, for it would be only harrowing up your feelings needlessly, to tell you of my sufferings. The weather meantime changed from bad to worse, and the motion of the vessel increased. So bad was it, that I made no effort to leave my bed until we had been out five days. We left on Saturday, and it was not till Thursday that I ventured to rise. It was then blowing a gale of wind, but I was determined to see at least one Atlantic storm, and accordingly got up, and dressed, though not without immense difficulty. After staggering along the passage and up the stairs, I sat down in the saloon, to rest; and gain breath and courage to complete my enterprise. The aspect of the main-deck, as seen from the saloon windows, was not encouraging. Spray was flying in showers, rendering the deck wet and slippery, and every now and then, as the ship rolled more heavily than usual, a huge leaden-coloured expanse, streaked and spotted with white patches of foam, became visible above the bulwarks. I was resolved, however, to see the scene on deck—and opening the door I crawled out, clinging to anything I could find, and getting wet through in my passage to the stairway. I succeeded so far as to get my head above the level of the spar-deck—and if you will refer to my sketch, you will have some idea of what I saw. Describe it, I cannot—I feel ill when I think of it. That exploit made me so sick, that I had to return to the solitude of my state cabin, nor was I able to leave it till the following Monday. On that day however the weather changed, and we were favoured with a sight of the sun, although it still continued rough, and the cold was intense. On going on deck, things looked much more lively than hitherto; almost all our passengers being assembled, some of them walking up and down, others gathered round the funnels, the neighbourhood of which was after all by far the most comfortable place. The decks looked beautifully clean, and nothing remained to tell of the gale, save the salt, which entirely covered both the funnels with a thick white coating. The day passed very pleasantly, and we had singing in the evening, in which some of the ladies joined. The next day was but a repetition of Monday; and we are now beginning to speculate as to the time of our arrival at Halifax. I shall here close this long epistle, and write again when we are fairly settled in our new abode. I had better leave this open, and if I have the time before the mail goes out, I shall add a line merely to tell you of our arrival.

## LETTER II.*

HALIFAX.

HERE we are at last, safe and sound. We did not, as is usual, sight Cape Race at all, so that the hills at the entrance of Halifax harbour were the first land we saw. But as I have brought our voyage down to Wednesday only, I have been rather too precipitate in bringing our good ship so soon to the end of her voyage, for when we retired to rest on Thursday night, there was no sign of land. At eight o'clock on Friday morning, our thirteenth day out, the steward came into our cabin with the welcome intelligence that we had entered Halifax Harbour. We rose and dressed with all speed—and as I was passing up the staircase—I felt the motion of the vessel cease: our voyage was at an end. I had been prepared for a wintery scene, but certainly my first view of Halifax gave me an idea of dreary desolation, infinitely greater than any thing I had previously imagined. I shall try to describe it,

---

\* All personal details of my residence in Halifax are purposely omitted; firstly, because to the general reader, they would be possessed of no interest; and secondly, because I feel that to make them public, would be very like a breach of that hospitality, which was so liberally extended to me there, and the remembrance of which will write "Halifax" in golden letters, in my memory for ever.

but I almost despair of conveying to you the impression it made on me. You must fancy yourself standing on a deck at least six inches deep in snow, and looking over the stern railings which were encased in a thick covering of ice. The harbour which is here about a mile broad, and was now frozen over, formed the centre of the picture; its smooth white surface being intersected by what looked like a narrow river full of floating ice, but was in fact the channel which we had broken in our passage up. It was far too thick, from mist and falling snow, to see the entrance of the harbour, distant about five miles, and the view was consequently limited to a circle of less than a mile. Close alongside on the right hand was the wharf at which we were preparing to make fast. On it were some thirty or forty people, all looking half awake and torpid, as well as about half a dozen sleighs, the jingling of whose bells, together with the blowing off of our steam, and the orders given by the officers, &c., were the only sounds audible. Indeed it seemed as though the whole place were in a state of hybernation. Along the margin of the harbour lay a long line of wharfs stretching as far as the eye could reach, and alongside of them numbers of small vessels all fast asleep in the ice. Behind these rose up the snow-covered roofs of the houses—with an occasional spire (looking black and grimy by contrast with the dazzling white of everything around) to break the monotonous outline, while the whole was topped, by the citadel, the very flag on whose staff seemed to have joined in the general slumber. On the left hand side of the harbour, the town of Dartmouth might have been discovered by any one who knew where to look for it, though the only indication of its whereabouts was a dirty-looking patch on the white hills which bounded the ice in that direction. Having comforted myself by a careful study of this very cheering landscape, I proceeded to get my effects on shore, and I and my friend soon found ourselves, standing sentry over our possessions in a shed on the wharf, there to await the usual and customary nuisance. We were the more annoyed when we found that the examination was a mere form, not one of our boxes being opened— not that I should have been better pleased, had everything been turned out, but when one is kept waiting, it is as well that it should be for something. My feet (having already passed through a dozen progressive stages of torture) by this time had ceased to remind me of their existence; indeed it required ocular demonstration to assure me that I still retained even boots—and accordingly, I determined to walk to the hotel, thereby hoping to infuse a little heat into my system. With this view, I engaged the services of the most respectable looking sleigh-driver I could see, and desired him to put our effects on his sleigh, and then drive slowly up to the "Waverly Hotel,"—going at a walking pace, so as to enable us to follow him. The result of this elaborate direction on my part, was, that having carefully attended to the first half of my injunction, the rascal rendered void the second, by starting off at full trot, disappearing round a corner, and leaving me to speculate on the chances which might exist, as to my ever seeing my "impedimenta" again. By dint of enquiry however, we soon found our way along the snow-covered streets, to the Waverley—and on arriving there, were greatly relieved by seeing our friend and his sleigh standing at the door. I was so thankful to find myself again in company with my effects, that I forbore to deliver myself of the very strong language which was on my tongue, and after some little trouble, we secured a comfortable room with (what appeared to be rather uncommon in the house) an open fire-place.

As you say that you wish to know exactly what sort of place Halifax is, I shall in this letter give you a description of the town itself, which will be helped out I trust by my drawings. The harbour of Halifax is nearly two miles wide at the entrance, and after extending inland for about four miles, divides ; one arm running beyond the point of division about a mile and a half further inland. The other, which is the principal portion of the harbour, after containing about an equal distance contracts to a very narrow channel, and then widens into a lake three miles long, known as the basin. The town of Halifax stands near the head of the tongue of land which divides the two arms of the harbour, being built along the edge of the principal one, just outside the channel leading to the basin. The distance across to the smaller or north-west arm is about a mile and a half at this point, and the town *may* perhaps some day extend quite across—at present however, it confines itself to one water front, and the wharves, &c. stretch for nearly two miles along the base of the hill, on which the town stands. In the harbour are two islands—the larger close to its entrance known as Macnab's Island, being nearly two miles long and the smaller (which is *very much* smaller) lying opposite the town. This latter is fortified and is called George's Island. On the eastern side of the harbour (Halifax standing on the western side) is the small town of Dartmouth. Having thus given you a general idea of the position of the city, I shall proceed to a more minute description. The citadel, occupying the summit of the hill, along the side of which the town is built, claims attention first. As you know, I have no acquaintance with military terms, but I shall do my best to describe what I saw, and you must not be too hard upon me. You enter through a stone archway, and after passing over the drawbridge, find yourself in a large court-yard. In the centre of this is a building, used as barracks, and containing in the upper part (which is a bomb proof), a large store of all kinds of murderous apparatus, such as shot, shell, gunpowder, &c. All round the yard are the quarters for the

officers and men. These latter are under the inner line of
fortifications, between which and the outer is a ditch. On
the angle facing the sea, is a small watch-house, with a powerful telescope, and close to it the flagstaff, from which the
arrival of the steamers, &c. is telegraphed. Passing underneath the inner line of bastions (or whatever the name of
them may be) you find yourself in a broad ditch, bounded
on each side by strong walls of masonry. Crossing this, and
entering a small door in the opposite wall, you discover a
long narrow passage, having loop-holes at intervals, commanding the ditch. The gallery extends entirely round the
citadel, and branching off from it at certain intervals, are
mines extending underneath the glacis. Altogether, it is an
interesting place to visit, especially when the tour of inspection is concluded by champagne in the officers' quarters.
Near the citadel, and on the slope of the hill, stands the
hospital—a long, ugly factory-like building and the Garrison Chapel, this latter being the regular old Pagan-temple
style. There is a very large and somewhat handsome building in course of erection, north of the town, which will be
used, I believe, for a barrack. So much for the military
establishment. The naval Dock-yard is at the extreme north
end of the city, nearest the basin, and in the summer time
there are generally three or four men-of-war stationed here,
one of them always being a line-of-battle ship. The city itself
extends along the shore for a distance of more than two
miles, and has an average breadth of three quarters of a
mile. It stands almost entirely on the slope of a hill—some
of the streets leading down directly from the citadel to the
water's edge being very steep, and affording in the winter time
a grand opportunity for the small boys to exercise their
favourite positions of "coasting." This process is achieved
by taking a small piece of wood about 3 feet by 2, placed on
runners; and walking with it to the top of the street, then

throwing it down and falling upon it. Of course, both boy and sled shoot down, at about fifteen miles an hour, regardless of sleighs that may be passing in the cross streets. This is a very favourite amusement, and is not by any means confined to boys. But to describe the city properly, we must begin at the north end, and take the route which would be pursued by any one arriving from the interior of the country. First we come to the railway station. This is the terminus of the only line as yet made in Nova Scotia, it extends to Truro, a distance of sixty-four miles, with a branch to "Windsor" on the Bay of Fundy, distant forty-five miles from Halifax.

Passing the station, the next prominent object is the Dock Yard, already mentioned, and here the town may be said to commence. It consists at this point, of two principal streets running parallel with the water, the inner one being of course on a much higher level than the outer. These continue for about a mile, and then sub-divide into four, and eventually five parallel streets. In the upper street, the first building of any pretension is St. Patrick's Roman Church, and nearly opposite St. George's Anglican Church.

I merely name these now, as I intend to devote another letter to an account of the ecclesiastical buildings and doings of Halifax.

Further on in the same street are a Baptist Meeting house, and the Garrison Chapel. In Water Street (the lower one) there is nothing to excite attention except Cunard's wharf, which lies just below St. George's Church. Passing on we come to where the streets divide.*

---

* This part of the town has, since my first visit, been almost entirely destroyed by a great fire. The result will, however, be in the end beneficial to the city, for instead of the wood which has hitherto been the favourite building material, the new houses will be of brick or stone, some of them being faced with white marble.

This is the chief business-part of the town, and some of the stores are quite handsome. The three principal streets at this point, are (beginning near the harbour) Hollis Street, Granville Street, and a third whose name I forget, but which is the longest and best of the three. Between Hollis and Granville streets, stands the Province building. In this place the provincial parliament meets, there being an upper and lower house. The building itself is a very plain Grecian edifice of grey stone, and is thought a great deal of by the Halifax people, though it always struck me as being frightfully ugly. Near this and close to the water is the market, a very commodious brick building, and close to it the ferry to Dartmouth. Hollis Street extends about a mile further, but contains nothing of interest save the Bishop's residence. I shall therefore follow the upper street which my faulty memory has robbed of its name. First comes a Scottish Free Church, and further on an open square bounded on the east side by the street, and on the west by the citadel hill. The Post Office occupies the north end, and St. Paul's Anglican Church the south. In the centre stands the Firemen's Station-house. Passing St. Paul's, we come to the Waverley Hotel, and opposite to it is a building known as Free Mason's Hall. Here is also the Roman Archbishop's residence, together with St. Mary's Roman Cathedral, and a House of Mercy. Higher up the hill and behind these is a somewhat pretty Presbyterian place of worship, which looks as though it were flinging defiance at the Roman colony beneath it. A little further on is another Presbyterian church apparently indulging in a similar display of ill-feeling towards the Bishop's house, which lies just behind it, in Hollis Street. I must not forget to mention two other buildings in process of erection.

One of them intended, I believe, for law courts, and the other as a monument to some Officers who fell in the Crimea.

They will both, I understand, be very handsome. Beyond this is the Government House, a plain stone building. This is the last public building in this direction, with one exception, which, in my reminiscences of Halifax will occupy a very prominent place, viz. *St. Luke's Anglican Church. This part of the town is composed entirely of private dwellings. Most of these are of one type, being small, two-storied houses built of wood, and painted white. They are very warm and comfortable, indeed the people seem to think them warmer than stone houses. I must not forget to mention the two cemeteries which lie to the west of the town, one of them having a pretty little chapel in it. To the west of the town are some pretty villas, &c., some of them being pleasantly situated near the north-west arm. The country is very well wooded, and in summer time many beautiful walks and drives may be enjoyed near the town.

Indeed, I can well believe that, (as every one tells me) Halifax is in summer one of the most delightful places imaginable. There is always abundance of gaiety, and the numbers of Military and Naval Officers give a tone of great liveliness to the society. Indeed the place is proverbial for its hospitality, and with great justice, as I can from personal experience bear witness, though like all towns of its size (population 40,000) it is by no means deficient in the article of scandal.

* St. Luke's has since been made the Cathedral Church.

## LETTER III.

HALIFAX.

As I have not much to tell you about myself, I purpose devoting this letter to an account of Ecclesiastical Halifax, and I shall describe the buildings, before speaking of the doings of those who worship in them. There are three Anglican churches, St. Paul's, St. George's and St. Luke's, besides a conventicle, which the good Bishop has hired for a Missionary chapel. St. Paul's, which is the oldest and ugliest, is (by courtesy) the Bishop's Cathedral. It is an oblong wooden box, with a thing very like a pigeon house, stuck on the top of a Brobdignagian inkstand, doing duty as a bell tower. The bells, however, are by no means bad. Internally, there is some attempt at decency and order. There are pews of course, and galleries all round; but the pews are not very high, nor are the galleries offensively hideous. Over the altar is a window, and in front of it is the pulpit. I have seen a Priest standing on the altar and pulling down the blind of the aforesaid window. On one side of the pulpit is the Governor's pew, and on the other, the Rector's. In the gallery at the end, stands an organ, fair to look upon, but most painful to hear. The case is evidently an old "Harris," so are the front pipes which (by the way) never speak now; but the interior is a mass of rubbish for which the parish paid a London organ builder £500 about twenty years ago, and which would be dear (save as old metal) at £50. St. George's church was built as a Garrison Church by the late Duke of Kent, and is also a wooden building. It is very peculiar in shape; being perfectly round with a dome in the centre. There are galleries of course, but as they appear to belong to the structure itself, they are not at all so offensive as such appendages generally are. Opposite the entrance stands a very good organ, in a gallery which occupies a recess, and in front of the organ come, in regular succession like a flight of stairs, the pulpit, the reading desk and the font. Is this emblematic of the relative importance of preaching, prayer and lastly, sacraments? One would think so, for the position of the altar carries out the idea to perfection: it is behind the pulpit and absolutely invisible from every part of the church. The organ is a fine one by Walker—it has 2 rows of keys and 25 stops, with 16 foot open pedal pipes. The pipes are diapered in blue and gold and the case altogether is very handsome. The Bishop's chapel is a specimen of the well-known style of conventicle, and is adorned with the word SALEM printed in huge gilt letters over the door. How some of its original proprietors would stand aghast, could they hear the sound catholic sermons preached there now, by the worthy Bishop! or see the beautiful cross of evergreens which decorated the wall above the altar at Christmas and Easter. I should be doing these excellent people great injustice were I to omit all mention of what was the glory of the place in their days. I have seen many pulpits, but I never saw one that could be mentioned in the same day with the one in Salem, for vastness. It is a costly thing too, being entirely of polished rosewood. In front of this erection stands the temporary altar, with a prayer-desk on one side, and a harmonium on the other. I now come to speak of S. Luke's,* and I do so with feelings of real interest —I might almost say affection—not that the building itself is such as to inspire any such feelings, nor even the services held in it—but, to the family of its most excellent rector, I owe a debt of gratitude, which never can be paid, for their continued kindness to me during the whole time of my residence here. St. Luke's church is, like the others, a wooden structure, but in designing it, a much greater regard has been paid to the proper ordering of a church than in the cases of St. Paul's and St. George's. The style is an imitation of mediæval, and considering all the circumstances, it might have been far worse. At the—I was going to say west-end, but the church stands north and south, so I must say at the entrance end, is a tower and spire—the latter being crowned by a very large gilt cross, which is no weather-cock and evidently points but one way. So persistently does it point, that several conspiracies dire have been formed against it by some of the crosshating and zealous Protestants of Halifax—but somehow there it is still, pointing out the way to Catholic truth most obstinately. On entering the church you are refreshed by a glimpse of a very fair sized altar. Not a very distinct or decided view, but still a glimpse. There are galleries, of course, but they are not by any means obtrusive, appearing to be, as in truth they are, a part of the structure. The pulpit stands a little on one side, as does the prayer-desk, thus allowing the congregation to see the altar, if they care to look at it. In the gallery over the door is a very fine toned organ by Walker. It has 2 rows of keys and 16 stops, and though not so large or powerful as the one in St. George's, is sweeter in tone. St. Luke's exhausts the list of Anglican

---

* Since my visit to Halifax, St. Luke's has been made the Cathedral of the Diocese. The structure has been enlarged by the addition of a large chancel; and the Rev. W. Bullock, the rector of my days, is now the Very Rev. the Dean of Halifax. A regular chapter has moreover been organized, and although in appearance St. Luke's may fall short of our Indian Cathedrals, it is in all essential points far more of a Cathedral than they are.

churches, and I have described it last, because it is the best. Now to describe the Roman churches. There are two of these, St. Patrick's and St. Mary's, the latter being (by courtesy) the cathedral. St. Patrick's is a large cruciform church, built of wood, and in no style in particular; it has a spire with a gilt cross, which looks like the twin brother of that on S. Luke's. Never having been inside, I cannot very well describe the interior, and shall therefore pass to S. Mary's. Externally this is the most hideous church in Halifax, but inside it is about the best. It is built of stone, and has stone columns supporting a plaster vaulting. There are galleries, and the whole design is very bad; but still there is an air of solidity about it and a church-like appearance, which is sadly wanting in the other churches. The altar is unfortunately very gaudy and tinselly as is too usual in Roman churches. There is a most terrible instrument of torture in the gallery over the door which does duty as an organ. There are several Presbyterian places of worship, the newest of which (near the Bishop's house) is by far the best looking building of the kind in Halifax. It is built of brick and plastered, but the mullions, &c. of the windows are of stone and the general effect is by no means unpleasing. The door is decidedly good, and the spire is admired by a good many people, though I confess it did not please me. And now I must say a few words about the church in Halifax, as a body. It has to contend with much opposition from Presbyterians, &c. and therefore great allowance must be made, but when the present Bishop first came, it must have been in a terrible condition. He has done a great deal, and is ably assisted in his good work by some of his clergy, of whom I must mention the Rev. W—. B—. of St. Luke's and his son the Rev. H—. B—. But there is a most determined spirit of opposition to fight against, and it is displayed chiefly by the churchwardens &c. I do believe that there is not, in the world, any society of men professing to live under a certain system, and systematically and deliberately acting in opposition to all the requirements of that system, in an equal degree with the great mass of those who profess allegiance to the Anglican church. But enough of this; it is a dangerous subject to meddle with, and had better be left to more experienced heads than mine. The services in these churches are all pretty much alike, at least those held in St. Paul's and St. George's strongly resemble each other. It is the regular last century style with the "Te Deum" read. At St. Luke's the "Te Deum" is sung, and on Easter Sunday I (having volunteered as organist) contrived to get up the Hallelujah chorus, and it was very well sung. For the present, you will probably feel that I have cantered far enough on my ecclesiastical hobby, so I shall dismount, though I don't promise not to give you another ride on the same steed at a future period. The winter is now nearly gone, and early in May, E—. and I think of starting for the United States. Though I don't much like cold weather, I look back on my winter here with feelings akin to regret. Indeed the winter of Halifax is one of its most peculiar features, and I saw it in full perfection. It is (when you have become used to it) very pleasant. I know nothing more enjoyable than a good sleigh ride. It is true the cold is intense, but then you are well wrapped up in furs and warm clothes, so that you do not feel it. If H. is inclined to doubt this, you may tell her that I suffered much less from cold in Halifax, than I have frequently done at home. The snow sometimes falls to the depth of three or four feet in a single night. The harbour frequently freezes, though not often entirely across; it did so however this winter, and the steamers had some difficulty in forcing their way up. On one occasion, I saw the "America" come up, breaking the ice as she came, whilst close to her, numbers of skaters were to be seen; it was a fine clear moonlight night, and the scene was really beautiful. My next letter will be written from Boston, U. S., as my present intention is to make that town my first resting place in the states.

## LETTER IV.

Boston, U. S.

WE left Halifax in the "Canada," on Wednesday last at three o'clock. I mention the hour, because it is a peculiarity attendant on leaving Halifax for the United States, that you never know, at what hour you may have to start. As you are aware, the Liverpool steamers touch at Halifax, to take up passengers for the States, and of course you cannot calculate the time of their arrival with any certainty, and we *might*, for aught we knew to the contrary, have had to take our departure in the middle of the night. Nothing of consequence occurred on the passage, there being of course the usual surfeit of lobsters, which a visit to Halifax always produces at the lunch table. Apropos of lobsters at Halifax, I heard a story, which well illustrates their exceeding abundance, and consequent cheapness. A regiment has just arrived in the town, and one of the officers, while passing through the market, on his way to the barracks, noticed the numbers of fine lobsters exposed for sale. On reaching his quarters, he despatched his servant with instructions to buy two pounds worth of lobsters, expecting to receive ten or a dozen. In about ten minutes the servant returned, followed by a man, wheeling a large barrowful of the creatures, and on his master expressing his amazement at such an "embarras de richesses," he burst out with, " Oh, Sir, that's not half. There's five more wheelbarrows coming." I think I hear H. exclaim, in imitation of Carlyle, " What a reservoir of lobsters to ride into!" But to return to our voyage. Coming on deck about 8 o'clock on Friday morning, I found the ship entering Boston harbour. The navigation appeared to be very intricate, we kept turning and twisting in amongst a number of smooth, round topped, green covered islands, until at length we saw the city of Boston looming up before us. It was a lovely morning, and my first impressions of Yankee-land were decidedly pleasing. Boston has been called the Venice of America by reason of its very amphibious position, the city proper being separated from its several suburbs, and the suburbs from one another by branches of the harbour, which seems to possess as many arms as a cutle fish. The general appearance of the city is very prepossessing, as it is built round the base and up the sides of a hill, which is crowned by the cupola of the State-house. It chief suburbs are Charlestown, South Boston, and East Boston. The former of these contains the navy yard, and at the latter is located Cunard's wharf, at which the "Canada" had now arrived. We found the Custom House here, to be a very different thing from that at Halifax, although I must say the officials were not nearly so rude as our own generally are. The only way to ensure civility in the United States is to treat every one as your equal, and present your boxes to the inspection of the Custom House myrmidons with as much courtesy as though you were offering your cigar-case to your most respected acquaintance. By pursuing this line of conduct, I got through the ordeal without much trouble, and directing our boxes to be placed on a coach bearing the name of the " Revere House," we ensconced ourselves in the interior of the same vehicle. This coach was the first "institution" peculiar to the country, which I had yet seen. It was about the size and shape of the old fashioned "family coaches" which flourished twenty years ago, (and which held four or even five people comfortably), thereby forming a marked contrast to the vehicle under discussion: for in this case no fewer than nine persons were jammed into the interior, and arranged thus. Three were on each seat, and across the middle came another (moveable) seat, holding three more, with a strap to prevent the occupants from falling back into the laps of those behind them. Being at length packed in, off we started along a most shocking road, which gave to the vehicle a motion equal to that of a ship in a storm: indeed I have often felt almost *sea sick*, in one of these machines. After crossing a railway track we turned sharp to the left and driving under a covered way, came to a standstill. On inquiry, I found that we were on board the ferry boat, which was to take us across to Boston, Cunard's wharf being, as I before mentioned, in East Boston. If I abused the Hotel carriages, I must here change the tune and praise, very decidedly, the admirable ferry boats. They are 100 feet long and 40 feet broad on the deck, though much narrower in the water; the deck being carried out on each side beyond the outer edge of the paddle wheels, and gradually narrowing towards each end. It is in fact an extension of the sponson to the entire length of the ship, and in this manner all the American river steamers are built. With the exception of about 20 feet at each end, the deck is covered over, the huge walking beam of the engine working up through the centre, leaving a space on each side for vehicles, while outside this on each side, (is a large cabin) fitted with seats all round. On the roof are the two pilot-houses, in which the steersman is placed, there being one at each end. In this respect all American steamships are alike, having in every case, the steering apparatus placed near the bows of the vessel, and enclosed in a small raised house, with windows in front. The ferry boats are lit up at night by gas. The dock into which they run, is contrived, so as to enable vehicles, &c. to cross at all times with equal facility, the gangway accommodating itself to the rise and fall of the tide. Altogether these ferries and their boats (the system being the same all through the country) are perfect, and form excellent models for imitation. On landing from the boat we drove through a number of somewhat narrow and tortuous streets, looking much more like those of an English town, than I had expected to find here; indeed, we passed one or two houses that looked positively old: and at length stopped in a small open square in front of a huge grey stone building, having " Revere House" printed in large gilt letters over the portico. After paying our fare, (a most exorbitant one, viz. 75 cents., equivalent to 3 shillings each) we followed our luggage up the steps into a handsome hall, paved with marble, and proceeded to insert our names in the book at the clerk's desk. I then received a key with a number attached to it, and marched off, after the porter, who led the way with the luggage, up five flights of stairs, and along an apparently endless corridor to number two hundred and something. Having been previously told that the furniture of the bed-rooms in American hotels was frequently limited to a bed and spittoon, I derived considerable satisfaction from a survey of my room, which was very comfortably, I may say handsomely, furnished. Observing a printed notice nailed to the door, I read it, and learnt, that breakfast was served from eight to eleven; dinner from two to five; tea from six to seven, and supper from nine to twelve. After correcting the disorder of my toilet caused by the journey, I descended to the dining room, and ate my first meal in the Great Republic.

# LETTER V.

As you say, that you always like to know something of the external appearance of any place at which I am residing, I shall give you in this letter, as concise an account of the city as I can. To begin with our hotel. The Revere House is generally considered the best hotel in Boston; indeed I have heard some people say that it is not surpassed by any hotel in the States. The main entrance, is not on the ground floor, there being a broad flight of steps leading up to the door, but there is a smaller entrance below. Here is situated that most important part of an American hotel, the barber's shop. I am sure every American passes at least an eighth part of his waking hours, under the hands of the barber. Looking in, at any hour of the day, you may see the forms of sundry free and enlightened citizens, stretched out in a horizontal position, and undergoing all the multifarious tweakings, combings, and shampooings, in which consists their favourite enjoyment. The actual shaving forms, comparatively speaking, a very small part of the business, though even that, (I cannot exactly understand, or explain why) takes long enough. I never could get through the process in less than half an hour, although always dispensing with all extras. I have gone into the shop at 10 o'clock, and recognized a friend undergoing the operation, and on returning at a quarter past eleven, have found him in precisely the same position. Next to the Barber's domain is the bar-room; where can be had all manner of tempting drinks, such as no European has ever dreamed of. There are always plenty of customers here enjoying their sherry-cobblers, gin-slings, brandy cock-tails, mint julep, egg-nog, and a score of other beverages, whose taste is in general far sweeter to the palate, than are their names euphonious. On meeting a friend for the first time, or rather I should say on being introduced to a stranger, the first thing proposed is always, "Let's have a drink"—and off you march to the bar-room of the nearest hotel. And yet you do not often see people intoxicated—the fact being that while we condense *our* tippling into a jollification in the evening, an American spreads it over a larger surface, and does a *little* tippling all day, instead of a great deal at night. On the same floor with the bar-room, &c. are the baths, kitchen, and billiard room. Ascending now to the grand entrance, we have on the right hand side the reading room; a small square apartment with a desk running all round, on which are placed newspapers from all parts of the Union, and having in one corner an electric telegraph apparatus, by which messages can be sent direct to any part of the country. Next to this on the same side is the staircase, and clerk's office, and opposite to it the gentlemen's parlour, a very handsomely furnished room, about 40 feet long. The first time I went into this apartment, I sat down at the table and took up a book. It was a railway and steamboat guide, and contained, as an additional inducement to the public to travel, a full account, copiously illustrated, of all the fatal steam-boat explosions that had lately happened on the Mississippi. A very cheerful and instructive style of literature certainly. Next to this is the principal dining or rather eating room, a splendid hall at least 70 feet by 30 and 20 feet high. It is paved with black and white marble, and looks delightfully cool in summer. The hotel is built with a court-yard in the centre, and these apartments occupy one side, while on the other are drawing rooms and a smaller eating room for the exclusive use of ladies. The house contains I forget how many bed-rooms, but it is over 200, besides several very handsome suites of apartments. Besides the Revere House there are several other fine hotels in Boston, amongst which I may mention the Tremont House, which is owned by the same proprietor as the Revere. Indeed, Mr. Paran Stevens, the aforesaid proprietor, owns, I was told, several other magnificent hotels, viz., the fifth Avenue Hotel in New York and a very large one in Philadelphia. These huge places have both their advantages and disadvantages, and for any one travelling through the country as a stranger and alone, I think I prefer the system to ours. You always know too, exactly what you have to pay, 2½ dollars a day (about 10 shillings) including every thing except wines, &c. and washing; this latter being performed in the most expeditious way.

One of the very first things which strikes a stranger in the streets of Boston, or indeed almost any American city, is the street railway. The city of Boston itself being built with narrow crooked streets, is not very favourable to such a kind of locomotion, but they extend to all the suburbs, and are a very great convenience. The cars are like very large ominbuses, as far as the interior goes, but run on ordinary railroad carriage wheels. There is a door at each end opening on to a platform to which access is easily gained by two steps on each side, the whole car being low. The horses can be attached to either end, so that when the car has arrived at the end of its journey, the driver shifts his horses to the other extremity of the car, and himself to the other platform. The roof being continued out over the platform, serves as a partial protection from the wet or the sun. These cars are entirely different from the large cars used on the locomotive roads, and of these I shall speak afterwards. The very first day of my sojourn in Boston, I had to make use of these cars to go out to one of the suburban villages called Cambridge ; like another Cambridge, the seat of a University. The town itself is exceedingly pretty, the houses being for the most part villas, belonging to the wealthy mercantile men of Boston. The University, or Harvard College, as it is called, is a group of almost old looking red brick buildings, with a very handsome chapel and museum of stone. Indeed the buildings look altogether very much as if two or three of the smaller Cambridge or Oxford "Halls" had been stuck down any-how in the gardens of S. John's College of the first-named University—minus the classic Cam. The whole establishment belongs to the Unitarians, who are by far the most numerous sects of religionists in the state of Massachusets. The students of course wear no distinctive dress—nobody, who can possibly avoid it, does in America. Even the railway conductors will only wear a band round their hats with the word "Conductor" printed in very small letters, and even this distinction generally gets turned round to the backs of their hats, so that no one can see it. If you are in a dilemma as to whom you should accost as the conductor, you will generally hit on the right person, if you pick out the most expensively got-up man in the car. The Chapel of Harvard College is, as I before said, a handsome building, and I may add very ecclesiastical in its appearance. It is in the Romanesque style, and consists of a nave without aisles, and a circular apse. There is a handsome campanle at one corner, and a very bold massive porch. The interior is fitted up in a most church-like manner, the sittings being of carved oak and very low.

In a small gallery over the grand entrance stands one of the most splendid *modern* organs I ever saw or heard, and one which would do credit to any English builder. It is by Simmons and Wilcox of Boston. In the apse stands a table vested in *green velvet* with a superfrontal, &c., and altogether looking like a most correct altar : on each side are stalls.

Seeing a handsome prayer book on the communion table, I took it up, and found a mutilated edition of the Anglican Book of Common Prayer.* The Museum, I unfortunately did not succeed in seeing, so I shall pass on to describe, as well as I can, the Observatory. I received through my kind Halifax friends an introduction to Mr. Bond, the astronomer, a man whose talents have gained him a world-wide reputation, and he very kindly showed me all over the place. The chief curiosity is the enormous telescope, the largest refracting telescope I believe, in the world. As you may be as ignorant as I was of the exact meaning of the term refracting telescope, I may say that it is one through which you look directly at the object, while in a *reflector* you see merely the image, a much less satisfactory thing in my opinion. This huge instrument is so beautifully balanced, that although it is near 20 feet long,† and I forget how heavy, a touch of the finger will move it. I had the pleasure of seeing Saturn, Jupiter and the moon through it, as well as binary stars, &c., and had a better astronomical lesson than I could have learnt from fifty books. Amongst the other buildings of Cambridge I may notice the Anglican Church, "Christ Church." It is a timber building and was sent out, with its bells, &c. from England about the year 1740 ; forming one of many similar reminiscences of the colonial days of this great nation. Near the town is the beautiful cemetery of Mount Auburn. But to return to Boston. The city, being built entirely without

---

\* All this has however since been explained by the subsequent conversion to the Church, of the minister for whom the chapel was originally built.

† The object glass is 14½ inches in diameter.

plan, it is impossible to describe the positions of the different streets, &c., and indeed I doubt if such a detail would interest you. I shall therefore confine myself to an account of the principal buildings, churches and places of amusement. The most prominent building in the city, is the State-house, which stands on the summit of a hill at the head of a park, handsomely laid out, and well planted, called the Common. The building is certainly imposing, chiefly from its position, but partly also from its design, it having a handsome Corinthian portico, and a dome, about 180 feet in height. Within are chambers for the accommodation of the members of the Government: each state having its own Governor, Senate, and House of Representatives, and being capable of enacting laws, &c. quite independently of the National Congress at Washington. Not far from this is the Boston Athenæum, a really handsome and solid looking building, containing a gallery of paintings and sculpture. The Common is bounded on its lower end, by Tremont Street, and by pursuing this for a few yards we come to the Tremont Temple, a handsome building externally, and containing amongst other apartments a very fine hall, which is used for concerts and meetings of different kinds. At one end, concealed by an open work screen, is an immense organ by Hook of Boston, containing 70 stops. Besides this Hall there is in Boston another and much finer, viz. the Music Hall. I do not know the exact dimensions of Exeter Hall, or of this; but I certainly think the Boston Hall is an infinitely finer room than the London one. It is certainly far higher in the roof, being at least 70 feet high. There is at present a moderate sized organ, but a new one is being built by Walker of Lúdwigsburg, near Frankfort in Germany; which is to cost 35,000 dollars (7,000 pounds), and which is confidently expected to be one of the finest in the world. In this Hall oratorios are frequently performed by a choral society, and I believe they are in general very well done, though I never chanced to hear one. To return to Tremont Street; a little beyond the Tremont Temple stands a building formerly called the King's Chapel, known however now, as the Stone Chapel. Next to this is the Boston Museum, consisting of a large hall, something like that of the Polytechnic in London, filled with stuffed animals and curiosities, and a theatre. This latter is the real source of attraction, no one ever seeming to bestow a look on the articles in the museum, the whole establishment furnishing a most instructive example of Puritan hypochrisy; and for this reason—Theatricals, being considered by the Bostonians of thirty years ago, infamous and disgraceful, of course no one had the hardihood to open a *regular* theatre and call it a theatre; so they had a museum, at which dramatic performances were allowed to form part of the exhibition, and thus paved the way gradually for the introduction of the drama, as an institution. In the theatre under consideration, I have seen some very good acting, infinitely better than could be had with us for the same price. The auditory of the American theatres is arranged very differently from ours, the pit (or parquette as they call it), and the first circle, being comfortably cushioned, and priced alike, viz. 50 cents. (about 2 shillings), with a small number of orchestra stalls at a dollar.

The "Howard Athenæum," for though *called* an Athenæum, it is nevertheless a theatre, is situated close to the Revere House, and generally can boast of a very good company. Besides these two, there is one other theatre in the city, the Boston Theatre in Washington Street. This is one of the most splendid buildings of the kind I ever saw, being very nearly equal in point of size to the New Theatre at Covent Garden in London, and quite equal to it in point of elegance: the entrance staircase is beyond comparison finer than any in London. Here operas are performed every now and then, and generally with first rate artists. I heard Don Giovanni, (with Formes as Leporello) splendidly performed in this theatre as well as Norma, and three or four of the most celebrated operas. Washington Street, in which the Boston Theatre stands, is the principal thoroughfare of the city, and contains some handsome shops, &c., but is very narrow and crooked. Amongst the prominent buildings of Boston, I must not forget to mention the Custom House, which stands near the wharfs, and like most of the buildings in that part of the city is built of solid granite. The interior is very handsome, there being a great appearance of strength and solidity, combined with considerable elegance of design. The roof is entirely of granite, and all the floors as well, I believe, thus rendering the structure completely fire-proof. You will see from this letter, how diligent I have been in sight-seeing, and I even managed to devote a day to the dock-yard this week, located at Charlestown. There seemed to be very little going on, and the whole had a very deserted aspect. There was an old three-decker, the "North Carolina," apparently rotting afloat, and a still older one, the "Vermont" rotting ashore. This latter indeed was not finished, but stood in dreary solitude on the stocks, reminding me more of the National Monument on the Calton Hill in Edinburgh, than of anything else. I have read, however, that the poor old thing is to be finished and launched after waiting some forty years for the ceremony. I believe they are going to make a steamer of her, although I can scarcely understand how a go-a-head people like the Yankees can expect to make such a terrible old tub do anything but shake herself to pieces with the machinery. It seems, however, that they are no better off in America with regard to their navy matters than we are—it is the same story with both: while our Mercantile Companies turn out such ships as the "Great Eastern," the "Himalaya" or the "Persia," the navy has not a ship to compare to either of the three; and while New York merchants have produced a superb vessel like the "Adriatic," the United States navy are all staring at each other, and wondering how it is that the "Niagara" leaks horribly every now and then, and will only go 8 knots an hour. Not far from the navy yard is Bunker's Hill, a spot which must suggest many grave reflections to every Briton who visits it. A monument of granite, in the shape of an obelisk, having a stairway inside, lighted by loop-holes, through which you may obtain a fine view of the city and harbour, commemorates the victory gained by the Americans at this place over the British forces; during the struggle for independence.

## LETTER VI.

BOSTON.

THIS is the last letter you will receive from Boston, as I intend starting for New York, in a couple of days; and I shall therefore send you to-day, a sort of supplement, to the description of this place, which I gave you in my last. You are I think aware, that the prevailing form of religion in Boston is Unitarianism or Universalism. There are but few churches of either the Anglican or Roman communions, and in those of the former persuasion which exist, there is an almost total absence of all ritual. One exception, however, must be made, and it deserves special notice,—I refer to "The Church of the Advent." Here there is daily prayer, morning and evening, and a celebration of the Holy Eucharist on Sundays and Festivals; the services being for the most part choral. The congregation occupy a wretched building at present, but funds are being collected for the erection of a new church. Even in the temporary church, there is, however, a permanent altar, of white marble, very unanglican, though costly and handsome, and having behind it a large gilt cross. There is one great drawback to one's satisfaction, in the otherwise well-conducted services—the boys are not surpliced, and the result is, of course, very unchurch-like and irreverent.

Considering however the general state of things in the Diocese of Massachussets, one must not be too critical, but give the "Church of the Advent" its due meed of praise as being the only attempt (in Boston at least) at a ritual service. The Bishop's Church is "Trinity." It is situated in Summer Street, near Washington Street, and is built in a very extraordinary style of architecture, peculiar to the country. I cannot possibly describe it, but my sketch may give you some idea of its general features. It is at all events far preferable to the ginger-bread gothic which prevailed in this country some thirty or forty years ago. The interior is very dark, there being no East window, and the side windows being quite obscured by hideous galleries. The organ is a large one by Gray and Davison of London, and exhibits all their usual harshness in the chorus without their peculiar sweetness in the solo and reed stops. The service is of course of the last century type, the Bishop appearing as often in his black gown as in anything else. Next in importance to this church is S. Paul's in Tremont Street, a Grecian building without any attempt at a church-like appearance. The interior however is much better than "Trinity," for there are no side galleries, and there is an apse with a fine large altar. The organ is in a gallery over the door, and is a very fair instrument by Hook of Boston. It is of large size, and is enclosed in a most magnificent case, with 16 feet speaking front. The choir is (as in most of the American churches) merely a quartette, but the organist, Mr. Wilcox, is fortunately a thorough churchman, and besides this, is one of the most beautiful players I ever heard. There are besides these several other churches, the names of which I now forget, with the exception of one in South Boston, S. Mathew's, the Priest of which was a very kind friend to me. Of the Roman Churches, I know but little, having seen only two, the Cathedral (a most wretched place) and one in Broadway, South Boston. They are, however, about to erect a new Cathedral in Washington Street, and the old one is to be pulled down. Of course, there are numbers of Unitarian places of worship, but I shall mention only one, the Stone Chapel in Tremont Street. This was, before the revolution, called the King's Chapel, and belonged to the Anglican Church. How the Unitarians have got hold of it, I can't conceive. It is a Grecian building, and contains a fine old organ by " Harris," which was sent out as a present by George the First. There is still the old Altar, used now as a communion table, and moreover, with very nearly the same liturgy, of course with considerate mutilation. In fact, I believe they are obliged to use the Book of Common Prayer, as the condition of their retaining the building. How they contrive to swallow some parts of it, I can't imagine. On the whole, matters ecclesiastical are, as will be perceived, at a very low ebb in Boston, although I trust a better day is coming; some twenty years ago the Church of the Advent would have been a sheer impossibility; and although it still stands alone, yet there is great progress being made. There is, in connection with the church a sisterhood, and I believe their numbers are increasing and their work beginning to have its effect. Though rather pressed for a time, I cannot finish this letter without mentioning the very great perfection to which they have brought their fire alarms. There is a central fire station from which, by means of telegraphic wires the bells of certain churches can be rung, there being a different mode of ringing to denote each portion of the city, and, branching from the above-mentioned central station are wires extending all over Boston and its suburbs. In every street, there is a small iron box fixed to the wall of one of the houses, and inside is an apparatus for communication with the central station by means of the wires; so that in case of a fire, say in Broadway, South Boston, you run to the nearest box, press a little knob inside, which gives the alarm at the central station; and from thence by means of the bells to the firemen; so that the engines are always on the spot within five or ten minutes of the first alarm. This excellent system, however, cannot be nearly so much needed in Boston, as in most other American cities, as it is, I hear, comparatively free from fires. Indeed Boston stands quite alone in several other important matters, not least of which, is its quietness and freedom from *rowdies*. It being almost the only city of any size in the country in which the streets are perfectly safe at night. With regard to climate, Boston is pleasant in the summer, by reason of the cool sea breeze, but it is fearfully cold in the winter, although the frost is seldom intense enough to freeze the harbour entirely across. This has indeed happened but twice since the establishment of the Cunard line of steamers in 1843, and on both occasions a channel was cut for the vessel to pass through, for the "Britannia" in 1844, and the "Arabia" in 1856, the Bostonians, showing a remarkable lack of Yankee sharpness on the latter occasion, having (with inconceivable stupidity) cut for the "Arabia" (of 2,400 tons) a passage of exactly the same width, as the one they had previously cut for the "Britannia," (of 1,200 tons). We leave this on Friday, and I shall write again as soon as I can after we reach New York.

## LETTER VII.

NEW YORK.

WE left Boston last Friday at five in the afternoon, by an express train, which took us as far as Fall River, (a distance of about 50 miles) and we were there transferred to the Steamer "Metropolis," which sailed at seven the same evening, and arrived in New York early the following morning; but before telling you of my journey, I shall describe the cars and locomotive. The cars are not, (like our carriages) divided into compartments, but are entirely open from end to end, about sixty feet long, and capable of containing some fifty-six persons. The seats, (each intended to be occupied by two travellers) are ranged in two rows, with a passage up the centre of the car, between the seats, the backs of which are moveable, so that if you prefer it, you can sit with your back to the engine, though (in their normal condition) all the seats face the engine. There is a door at each end of the car, both of which open on small platforms; similar to those on the horse cars, I described to you, in one of my letters from Boston. When the cars are coupled together, you can pass from one end to the other with perfect ease. They are lighted at night by two lamps, and warmed by a stove at each end. A smoking car is generally attached to each train. It differs from the others, in having two or three card tables and (instead of cushioned seats) chairs turning on a pivot, its furniture also includes an innumerable multitude of spittoons. The cars are also frequently lighted by gas!

The body of the car is supported on two trucks, one at each end, leaving the centre of the huge long affair entirely unsupported: by this arrangement they are enabled to turn almost at a right angle without going off the track, the forward truck being frequently at that angle with the hinder one. The motion is delightful, on account of the capital arrangement of springs, &c.,and if the roads were only decent, the travelling would be all that can be desired, but smooth railways are unknown in America. One of our railway carriages with its four or six wheels set in one rigid frame, would not go 300 yards on an American road without running off the track; while a car made in the American fashion, would run on our splendid roads without the smallest danger of leaving the rails, and with a motion which would be quite imperceptible to the passenger. The locomotives generally have four large driving wheels, six feet in diameter, and are supported in front on a small four-wheeled truck, similar to that used for the cars. The driver and fireman have a comfortable roof over their heads with large plate glass windows in front of them. Besides the whistle, (generally a much larger one than with us) there is always a bell, which is rung when passing through a town (which the railways here do on a level and without any fencing.) Besides these points of difference from a European engine, there is the funnel, made of enormous size with a gauze covering to catch the sparks from the wood fire, and there is also the cow-catcher. In front of the funnel is a huge lamp, at least two feet square, which throws a brilliant light a considerable distance ahead, and is often the means of averting accident. Our journey to Fall

River was performed at a speed of about thirty-five miles an hour, the train being an express, and stopping but seldom. To me, one of the greatest drawbacks to the system seemed to be the continual opening and shutting of the doors. First, would come through, the conductor, then a boy with books, then another boy with eatables, and so on the whole way. The country was not by any means striking, although (for America) somewhat densely populated. We reached Fall River before seven o'clock, and at once embarked on board the steamer. And here I must again digress to describe these truly magnificent vessels. The "Metropolis" is one of a line of similar vessels, and indeed, when I describe her, I give a general idea of all American River or Lake Steamers. She is three hundred and fifty feet long and near sixty broad, that is on the main deck, although not so wide in the water, by reason of the build, which is the same as that of the ferry boats described in a former chapter, this sort of continuous sponson being called in America "the guards." On the main deck is the ladies' saloon (at the extreme stern) and forward of this the deck is unencumbered, and available for cargo. The entrance gangway is just aft of the paddle wheels, and on entering you have, therefore, the ladies' saloon on one side, the staircase to the saloon above on the other, and opposite to you, the captain's office. Forward are the boilers, one on each side, poised as it were over the water, and with staterooms just above them! Above this deck is the principal saloon, extending the entire length of the vessel, excepting a small space of open deck astern, and another and larger, forward. There is no attempt at concealing the machinery which works up through the centre of the saloon, from which it is distinctly visible through large plate glass windows, and, being beautifully finished and kept perfectly bright and clean, is rather an ornament than otherwise. The furniture of the saloon is very handsome, consisting of chairs of every variety of shape, and tables, ranged down the centre of the room, the sides being occupied by the doors of the state rooms, which open off it. There is not much decoration about the structural portion of the room, and far too great a predominance of white paint. Indeed the whole vessel, outside as well as in, is painted white. I have noticed that the taste* of the people cannot discriminate, in decoration, between bald nakedness and chaste simplicity, or between vulgar gaudiness and gorgeous splendour. Below the main deck is another long saloon with berths (four tiers of them) on each side, and to this we descended for supper soon after our start. The saloon was brilliantly lighted by chandeliers, and a most abundant supply of food was on the table. After supper most of the male passengers made their way to the "bar room" (for there are a barber's shop and bar room on every steamer), there to "liquor" and talk politics. Not being minded to do either, I went out on to the open portion of deck at the bows, where the greater number of the lady passengers were assembled. I have not yet said a word regarding the external appearance of the vessel, and indeed, my sketch conveys a much better idea than words could possibly do. You will observe that the paddle wheels (forty feet in diameter) are considerably nearer the stern than the bows; this is the case I find with all American steamers, and is an improvement, to which we are only just becoming alive. The large house on the upper or hurricane deck is the pilot house, and contains the steering apparatus; while the enormous arches of wood, running along each side of the vessel, are braces to strengthen her. In fact, the structure would stand a great chance of falling to pieces in the first heavy sea, were it not for these braces, for these steamers are not by any means strongly built. Shortly after dark, being then in Long Island sound, we met a slight sea, which however made the

---

\* This is the case throughout America.

"Metropolis" roll and pitch in the most uncomfortable manner, more especially as the floor, sides, and roof of the cabin seemed each to be endowed with an independent motion of its own. I went to bed early and after a comfortable night, rose at seven o'clock and on emerging from the saloon on the forward deck, found that our vessel had passed "Hell Gate," and was close to New York. On the left hand side rose up the thickly built Brooklyn Heights, while in front extended the beautiful harbour, stretching away toward Staten Island, and on the right were the wharfs, and red brick warehouses of New York, above which rose up one tall and handsome church spire, which, I was delighted to find, belonged to an Anglican Church; on close scrutiny other spires could be seen, but on a first view of New York, Trinity Church is decidedly the object which most arrests the eye. Presently after rounding an abrupt point to the right, we found ourselves moored alongside a wharf, and at once prepared to land, a feat which was not accomplished without some difficulty, and at the imminent risk of being torn piecemeal by the porters, &c. on the dock. At last we found ourselves safe in one of the abominable hotel coaches already described. After driving a few hundred yards straight from the wharf, we turned sharp to the left, and passing on the right a small planted enclosure, entered an imposing, but somewhat narrow street. Could this be Broadway? I had pictured a street as wide as George Street in Edinburgh, nay wider, and planted with trees along the side walk, whereas this was barely wider than Oxford Street, London. But Broadway it was, and if disappointed with its width, I was most agreeably surprised at the imposing nature of the buildings. Presently we passed a large church on the left, which I conjectured, and rightly, to be Trinity; the little narrow street leading out of Broadway opposite to it, looking most unlike my previous ideas of that far-famed haunt of Mammon, Wall Street:

but such it was. A few hundred yards further on, you see on the right, a most extraordinary building, looking with its queer paintings between the numerous windows and the multitude of flags all over it, (not to mention a fearful brass band playing in a gallery over the door) just like some huge travelling show, suddenly petrified into stone. It needed not the name written in huge gilt letters on the front, to point this out as Barnum's Museum. Opposite to it is an almost old looking Grecian Church, and a large grey stone, many windowed building, which we recognized from previous descriptions, as the Astor House. A little further on we passed a large white marble building surrounded with trees, and standing in an open space. This is the city Hall. Then succeeded rows of splendid marble buildings in all stages of progress interspersed with little mean looking brick houses, and after crossing a wide street, at the foot of which appeared masts and other indications of the water side, our coach drew up at the door of the S. Nicholas' Hotel. Here we went through the same process as on our first arrival at the Revere House, Boston, and afterwards sat down with sharpened appetites to breakfast for the first time in the Metropolis of the West.

## LETTER VIII.*

NEW YORK.

As I have already told you all about myself, I shall in this letter give you an account of New York. The city occupies at present the south western portion of Manhattan Island. The entire island is already laid out in streets and squares, the greater proportion of which are however still in embryo. It is separated from the mainland, on the North by the Harlem River (which however is rather a channel than a river) connecting the Hudson with Long Island Sound; on the west by the Hudson, while its eastern side is washed by the aforesaid Long Island Sound. It is, in fact, shaped very much like a triangle, and towards the south west, ends in a sharp point, at which, the junction of the North and East Rivers, (as the Hudson and the Sound are often called) form the harbour. The principal outlet to this harbour, is not through Long Island Sound, but lies to the south, between Long Island and Staten Island; another passage runs between Staten Island and the Jersey shore. The Staten

---

* I must here observe that all those parts of my letters containing personal details of my residence in America, are purposely omitted. I paid two visits to New York, on the first occasion remaining only a fortnight in the latter, taking up my abode there, for many months. The letters from New York contain the result of my observations during both visits, but I have not thought it necessary to specify the date, on which each letter was written.

and Long Island shores approach very near each other at this point, the passage between them being called "The Narrows," and defended by a Fort, distant about eight miles from New York. Beyond this, the harbour widens out, and after passing round a narrow neck of land, which stretches out from the Jersey shore (and is known as Sandy Hook) you are at sea. Close to Sandy Hook is the bar, and here the depth of water seldom exceeds twenty-nine feet, rendering it a somewhat difficult task to navigate very large vessels safely over, and always making it necessary to call in the aid of a pilot.

If however the entrance by Sandy Hook be such as to require care, how much more intricate is the navigation through Long Island Sound. The difficulty here is at the point when the Harlem River branches off, and was formerly so great as to render the passage almost impracticable, and to gain for it the title of Hell Gate. By dint however of blasting the rocks which obstructed the passage, it has been made navigable for craft drawing a small amount of water.* This approach to New York is not nearly so striking as the other. You miss altogether the beautiful bay, and the picturesque shores of Staten Island, which are all seen to advantage by any one arriving direct from Europe, and which make the approach to the city exceedingly imposing. On the right is the Long Island Shore, at this point well planted, and sprinkled with villas, and a little further on, the crowded wharfs, buildings and spires of New York; while on the left is Staten Island also well wooded, and with numbers of pretty residences overlooking the water; beyond it is the Jersey shore with the busy town of Jersey city (directly opposite New York), and farther on again the thickly planted

---

\* The wise people in charge of the unfortunate "Great Eastern" once took that noble vessel through Hell Gate, the result being that she struck, and tore a rent 80 feet long in her bottom.

heights of Hoboken. The centre of the picture is occupied by the glorious Hudson, which stretches far away inland till lost to sight amongst the hills which form a beautiful back-ground to the whole. Manhattan Island is about 12 miles long and nearly 4 wide, at the base of the triangle, that is, at its northern end; and the whole of this, with the exception of about two miles at the South, or "down town" end as they call it, is laid out on a regular plan, having numbered avenues running North and South with numbered streets crossing them at right angles. The main artery of the city is Broadway, and this commences at the extreme point of the island, from which diverge two other long streets, one on each water front.

As the island gradually widens out, of course more longitudinal streets become necessary; and first appear the Bowery on the East side of Broadway (from which it branches off at Barnum's Museum opposite the Astor House,) and West Broadway on the West side. These streets run nearly parallel about one mile further, when they are crossed by Canal Street, and a short way beyond this, the Avenues, and numbered streets begin, 5th, 6th, 7th, 8th, and 9th Avenues being on the West side of Broadway, and Bowery resolving itself into 4th, 3rd, 2nd and 1st Avenues. At tenth street Broadway turns slightly to the West, thus crossing 5th, 6th, and 7th Avenues in succession. The streets are numbered as far as 150th street, but they are only built up to about 42nd street. Having thus given you a general idea of the plan of the city, I shall commence serving it up in detail, and shall begin of course with Broadway. The extreme point of the island, between the North and East Rivers, is occupied by an open space, partly planted, but chiefly covered with dirt and dust, and called the Battery, because I suppose there are no guns. There is a queer looking erection at the water's edge, called "*Castle Garden,*" a name which conveys as much meaning of what the place really is, as though it had been called Mont Blanc. There certainly is no garden, nor have I yet discovered any castle, the place being chiefly known as a rendezvous for freshly arrived emigrants. Facing this is a small square, called the Bowling Green, which was once the residence of the fashion and wealth of New York, but is now occupied by almost entirely by steamboat offices. From this square opens Broadway and up this we shall now proceed, first remarking on the army of white omnibuses which completely block up the street.

Talking of omnibuses, the American ones are certainly far better than ours, simply because they are wider and, generally higher. There is no conductor, the driver receiving the fare through a little round hole in the roof, and controlling the door by means of strap, one end of which is fastened to it, and the other to Jehu's foot; so that when you wish to emerge, you have merely to pull the strap, and the door opens and the omnibus stops. I have often thought the poor fellow's ankle must be sore before the day is over. The buildings in the lower part of Broadway are mostly of brown stone and are very lofty, so much so as to make the street, which is not at all wider than Oxford Street, if so wide, appear much narrower than it really is. They have a terrible habit here too, of allowing cart loads of boxes and bales to accumulate on the side walk, and as it is at the risk of one's life to venture into the centre of the street, most people prefer either to wait; or clamber over the heap, which decidedly impedes the circulation of the crowd. The first building of importance is Trinity Church, which stands within a church-yard planted with fine trees, on the left hand side, and directly opposite to it is Wall Street. This is the great business-place of the city, and here are the Custom House and Merchant's exchange. It is a short narrow street leading down from Broadway to the East River. Of Trinity Church I shall tell you more by and bye, and will therefore say no more of it now. About quarter of a mile further on we come to the great focus of most of the traffic in the city. Here, Park Place leading to the Bowery and east side of the city, and Vesey Street leading to the west, branch off from Broadway. On the left in the corner of Vesey Street is St. Paul's Church, and just beyond it, on the further side of Vesey Street, is the Astor House, while opposite these, and at the junction of Broadway and Park Place is Barnum's Museum.

From this point start the horse cars for all the avenues, and here concentrate nearly all the omnibuses, causing inextricable confusion, which culminates just opposite Barnum's, where may be witnessed, every day, a performance popularly known as Barnum's quadrille. This is a most interesting spectacle, and I have seen half a dozen couples, at each side engaged in the dance. The pair generally consists of a timid lady and a valiant policeman, who often have to "chasser" into the middle of the street and back again five or six times before they can get across, the accompaniments being supplied gratuitously by the brass band on Barnum's gallery. Passing on, we have on the right an open space, planted with trees and dignified by the name of the Park, though the City Hall, which stands in the centre of it, occupies nearly its whole area. The building is of white marble, and did not strike me as in very bad taste, although every one abuses it. There is a cupola at the top crowned by a figure of justice, which was put up in defiance of the strong recommendations of the New York papers to substitute a weather-cock, as being cheaper and far more appropriate. Inside the building are held the Courts of Justice. Beyond this, on the same side, is the splendid white marble store of Stuart, at which may be bought everything except eatables; and a little further on, is the building belonging to Appleton, the great publisher. Near this, on the left hand side, is Taylor's Saloon, a huge restaurant, fitted up in the most frightfully gaudy style, and supposed to be gorgeous. I can't say much for it as an eating place either: everything is filthy, and I once had coffee brought me in a pot half filled with old tea leaves. The people too are a most horribly suspicious generation, the waiter always stands staring at you like a basilisk to see that you don't walk off with the spoons. But I do not quote Taylor's as by any means a specimen of New York restaurants. At Delmonico's you can get as good a dinner as any where in London, perhaps better. A little way beyond this, Canal Street crosses Broadway, leading to the right, into the Bowery, and to the left, down to the Hudson or North River. Most of the stores in this neighbourhood are superb, some of them are perfect palaces, far exceeding in appearance any in London. About 300 yards beyond Canal Street is Wallack's Theatre on the left hand side, and close to it on the same side, the S. Nicolas Hotel, of which more anon, and next to it is the Prescott House. Continuing, we have on the right the Metropolitan Hotel, nearly as large as the S. Nicholas, and containing within its courtyard a theatre known as Niblo's garden, and further on, Laura Keene's theatre, opposite to which is S. Thomas' Church. At this point an attempt has been made to preserve a few trees along the side walk, but the street is too narrow to allow them their proper effect. One thing which must strike a stranger very much, is the multitude of flags everywhere visible. Every hotel has three or four flying, and you continually find advertisements in the shape of flags flying from ropes stretched across the street. On the left, about quarter of a mile beyond S. Thomas' Church is the Lafarge House, and a little further on the other side in Astor Place, leading into the Bowery. The building which was formerly used as the Opera House, and which was the scene of a fearful riot on the occasion of Mr. Macready's performance, is located here, but is now used used for other purposes. A few yards beyond this is 10th street and here Broadway bends to the left. At the corner, on the right hand side, stands Grace Church with its parsonage. It is about three miles from the Battery to this point and (the street being perfectly straight,) the view either up or down is exceedingly fine, the spires of Grace Church at one end, and of Trinity at the other, forming beautiful terminations to the long vista of splendid buildings. Proceeding onwards for about quarter of a mile we reach Union Square, extending from 14th to 16th streets. It is nicely laid out with trees in the centre, and at one corner is an equestrian statue of Washington, in bronze. A little way up 14th street on the right is the Academy of Music, and on the further side of the square is the Everett House, a very good hotel. The Fourth Avenue railroad skirts the Eastern side of the square, and the only object noticeable on the Western side is the Meeting House of Dr. Cheever, one of the great antislavery agitators. His Church which was built after an idea of his own, pretty clearly proves by its design, his one-sided character. The front is (excepting detail) a sort of reproduction of some church which took the doctor's fancy in Europe, and has two towers, one half finished (apparently.) This was thought to be highly picturesque, and certainly has the merit of being an entirely original idea. Between this and 23rd street, there is nothing worthy of remark, save the extreme badness of the pavement, which was full of most dreadful ruts and holes, and caused vehicles to jump about in such a manner as to render the retaining of one's seat, a matter of difficulty. At 23rd street Broadway crosses Fifth Avenue, obliquely, and here also, extending from 23rd to 26th street is Madison Square. Occupying the entire block between 23rd and 14th streets, and extending a considerable distance back into both streets, is the Prince of American Caravanserais, the Fifth Avenue Hotel; it is faced with white marble, and is seven stories in height, completely dwarfing Delmonico's new Hotel, on the other corner of 24th street. Beyond this there are few objects of interest in Broadway: it crosses 6th Avenue at 32nd street, and after intersecting 8th Avenue, merges into the Bloomingdale Road, and under different names extends as far as Albany, 150 miles off.

Although Broadway is the principal street in the city, it must yield the palm to Fifth Avenue as regards its appearance. In this street are some of the handsomest town residences of which any city in the world can boast. They are for the most part built of brown stone, and are of varied and frequently elegant designs. The street too is wider than Broadway, and at its lower end there are rows of fine trees along the side walks. Altogether the fifth Avenue of New York will bear comparison with any street in the world, and when it extends, as it eventually will, to a length of three miles, ending at the Central Park, will certain surpass any street which I, at least, have seen. In this comparison I do not include Prince's Street, Edinburgh, which I leave entirely out of the question, as being above and beyond all comparison. There are several handsome places of worship in the street, most of them belonging to the Dutch Reformed Church. Between 40th and 41st street is the reservoir of the Croton water, with which New York is most abundantly supplied. The water is brought to the city a distance of about forty miles, and the channel through which it flows is carried on embankments or through tunnels as far as the Harlem River, which it crosses by means of a splendid aqueduct nearly 1,500 feet long, and having fifteen arches 180 feet high: from this point to New York the ground is nearly level. The water is very good, but one's comfort in using it is much affected by the quantities of insects called " Crotonbugs," which always infect its neighbourhood. At present, Fifth Avenue forms the central abode of the elitè of New York, the fashionable quarter extending along its entire length, and through the cross streets on each side into Madison Avenue which runs parallel with it: in a few years however I expect that the lower part of Fifth Avenue will be given up to shops, as there is a steady move gradually further "up town," which has been going on ever since the city was built. The rents of the houses are perfectly exorbitant, as much as 2,000 dollars a year, (£400) being given for a house, which might easily be rented even in London for £150, and in Edinburgh for £80 or 90. The houses are handsome and commodious, but I do not think, very substantially built, their safety too is constantly imperilled by the tremendous fires which are always, in the winter time, kept blazing in the furnaces, and if one house catches fire, "next door" is pretty nearly sure to follow. In these cases however, there is little danger to the inmates: as the roof generally affords an opportunity for escape, when retreat by the door is cut off; but in the poorer parts of the city, where "tenement houses" abound, the loss of human life is most fearful. These vile mantraps are built in the most reckless, careless manner, and run up to a height of frequently seven and eight floors, without any means of escape, save perhaps one staircase. Several instances have occurred, since I came here, of fires originating, close to the staircase in houses, such as I have mentioned, and the result in almost every case, was frightful loss of life. I remember one night, during which there occurred in New York and Brooklyn, three fires, two boiler explosions and two or three fatal accidents at the docks, the whole being wound up with an execution early in the morning. In one fire fifteen persons perished, in another three, and I think some five or six were killed by the explosions, which both happened in Brooklyn. One of the great attractions of New York is the Central Park, which is in course of construction at the upper end of the city. As yet indeed, it is quite out of the town, and occupies a space extending in length from 60th to 100th street, a distance of two miles, and in width, from 8th to 5th Avenue, or about three quarter of a mile. Although, as yet, unfinished, it is possible to judge of its general appearance, and it will, when completed, form a most beautiful and picturesque Park. The lower end is laid out chiefly in broad drives, and gravelled walks, while the upper part is planted with shrubbery and contains pretty winding paths. This part is called the "Ramble." There is a large piece of water crossed at several points by very handsome stone bridges, and at the lower end of it, a set fountains and a cascade are in course of construction. The Park has already become the fashionable drive, and from 3 to 5 o'clock it is crowded by the vehicles of "Upper Tendom." In nothing do the Americans differ more from us than in the construction of their carriages, and although they certainly build them much lighter than we do, such a thing as an "equipage" is perfectly unknown. They seem to have but two styles of carriage; either a close carriage, with a large body hung on small light wheels, or a small open barouche; and no colour but black is ever used, making the close vehicles resemble mourning coaches, most painfully. Their light trotting wagons are very funny-looking things, with four spidery looking wheels all the same height, and the front and hind wheels not more than five or six inches apart, rendering it a matter of no small difficulty to get into the seat, which generally holds two persons. In these vehicles the "fast" portion of the New York community demonstrate their right to the title, by driving along the Bloomingdale Road at the rate of 18 or 20 miles an hour. Among the amusements of the city, the theatres of course occupy a prominent place, and in some of them the performances are of a very high character. The best company is to be found at Wallack's Theatre on Broadway: indeed, during the past year this company has been above the average of London theatres. I saw the "Overland Route" performed by them, and having seen it previously, as you know, at the Haymarket Theatre in London (at which it was first brought out), I must say the New York performance was beyond all comparison better than the London one, actors, scenery, and music, being alike superior. Besides this, there is Laura Keene's Theatre, also on Broadway, and here the performances are often very good, and the orchestra is one of the best I ever heard in any theatre. Niblo's Garden and the *Winter Garden are also very good theatres, the former being part of the same building as the Metropolitan Hotel, and the latter adjoining the Lafarge House. *The opera House or Academy of Music as they call it, is in 14th street, and is a fine large house, hardly equal however, in my opinion, to the Boston Theatre. The interior decoration struck me as being too heavy, and the entrance is abominable.† Besides the above mentioned there are also theatres in the Bowery, known as the Old and New Bowery theatres, but I never was inside either of them, the audience in general being of a somewhat "roudy" character. Barnum's Museum has also a theatre in connection with it, after the manner of the Boston Museum, though Barnum generally keeps the museum part of the establishment pretty prominently before the public. He is always getting up some kind of grand humbug or another, his latest effort being the procuring of an unfortunate little idiotic nigger, whose head he shaved, and whom he exhibits as a nondescript link between man and monkey. This "freak of nature" he has denominated the "What is it," the answer to which question

---

* Both the Winter Garden and Academy of Music have since been burnt.
† It was in this theatre that the grand ball was given to H. R. H. the Prince of Wales in 1860.

would be "Another of your unblushing pieces of humbug, Mr. Barnum." A story, for the truth of which I cannot vouch, is told of Mr. Barnum's uncommonly sharp practice. An advertisement appeared in the "Herald" to the following effect "Four dollars a week—to play four hours a day—a vacancy in Barnum's brass band offers an eligible opportunity for performers on the Cornet-a-piston." An applicant soon appeared, and was duly installed in the band. At the end of the week he went to Mr. Barnum for his four dollars, and the following conversation is *reported* to have ensued. Mr. Barnum: "Well, sir, I suppose you've called about your bill." Victim : "Yes, sir, here it is." Mr. Barnum : "Well I guess you've made a considerable mistake here. I don't owe you four dollars, no how you can fix it." Victim : "But indeed you do; you advertised for a player, and offered him four dollars a week." Mr. Barnum : "No, *Sirree*, I tell you I didn't. I offered you the use of my gallery to practice and blow away at your tarnal trumpet, so as you would'nt disturb any body with the row, and I guess you've had it uncommon cheap at four dollars, but if you cant pay why there's an end of it, so make tracks, and clear out." In the midst of a great deal of rubbish in the museum, I saw one or two interesting things, among others, a really good collection of aquaria. There is a great want of some large hall for musical or other meetings, such a thing as an oratorio is never heard, except on Christmas eve, when the "Messiah" is performed at the Academy of Music. The hotels of New York are both splendid and numerous, the finest being the Fifth Avenue, the S. Nicholas, the Metropolitan and the Astor, though some of the smaller ones such as the Everett House in Union Square, the "Clarendon," the "New York," or the "Brevort," are much more comfortable. The Fifth Avenue Hotel is a magnificent building cased with white marble, and contains accommodation for 1,200 guests. The principal eating room is a splendid hall, nearly square, and measuring, I should think, 100 feet across and from 20 to 30 feet in height. The drawing-rooms are all fitted up in the most expensive manner, and the effect of the decoration is very beautiful, although somewhat cold; nothing being employed but white and gold with innumerable mirrors. The basement stories of all these great hotels are occupied by shops, the owners of which pay an enormously high rent, but I suppose they find it a profitable transaction in the end. The St. Nicholas, at which I put up on my first arrival in New York, although not quite so large as the Fifth Avenue Hotel, is a splendid house. It is however frequented by a much less select style of company, and, (the bar-room especially) is frequently the scene of broils and disturbances, in which pistols and bowie knives are recklessly made use of. To do the New Yorkers justice however, the persons who indulge in this kind of pastime, are generally Southerners, and most frequently politics are the origin of the quarrel. I shall here bring this letter to a close, for though much more might be said about hotels, you have, I dare say, had enough of the subject.

## LETTER IX.

NEW YORK.

As H. entertains a mortal aversion to the very name of "ship" or "steamer," she need not read this letter unless she likes, for I give you warning that it is about ships that I am now going to write. One of my favourite lounges, is the line of wharfs, on the North or Hudson River, at which lie most of the steamers, the East River being occupied chiefly by sailing vessels. These wharfs are, in all cases, long piers built out into the river, and the vessels lie at either side of them, at right angles to the shore. I should think that no single port in the world can show at one time, such an assemblage of splendid steamships, as may be often seen here,* and besides the Ocean Steamers, there are always six or eight of the enormous Sound and Hudson River boats. As it may perhaps interest you, I shall follow the line of piers on the Hudson River beginning at Pier No. 1, at the Battery, and give some idea of the steamers sailing from each. First comes a line of steamers running to Providence, for Boston, starting every evening at 5 o'clock, and next to them is the

* I have seen the "Great Eastern," the "Persia," the "Asia," the "Adriatic," the "Niagara" and the "Vanderbilt," all in the harbour at the same time; besides several others above 2,000 tons; those I have named above, (the "Asia" excepted,) being the five largest steamships afloat.

wharf of the Fall River boats, the "Metropolis," "Bay State," and "Empire State." At the other side of the same pier lie Vanderbilt's European steamers, running from New York to Havre viâ Southampton. Of these the "Vanderbilt" is the largest and finest. She is a splendid vessel of about 3,000 tons of our measurement, though by the American method she is 3,350 tons. She is a very fine model, and is one of the fastest vessels afloat. She is lightly rigged with two masts, as are all the American steamships, and has two walking beam engines. Next to this is a line of fine steamers running to Charlestown and Savannah; and then follow numbers of sailing vessels. About half a mile up, are the Hudson River Steamers, leaving New York for Albany every evening at 6 o'clock, and reaching their destination early in the morning. There are two lines of these, one consisting of two fine steamers, the "Commodore" and "Francis Skiddy," while to the other belong the two largest river steamers in the world, the "Isaac Newton"* and "New World." To give some idea of the enormous size of these boats, I may state that the "Isaac Newton" is 400 feet long by 70 feet broad, and has 4 tiers of cabins. Her saloon is near 20 feet high, and has an arched roof in imitation of a stone vaulting, and is decorated in the "Strawbery Hill" Gothic style. There is a gallery running all round, from which access is gained to the upper tier of State-rooms. Her general construction is similar to that of the "Metropolis," though I should imagine that she is not quite so strongly built. The most beautiful saloon I saw on any of these boats, was that of the "Francis Skiddy." Like the "Isaac Newton's" it has a gallery running round it, but the roof is entirely of stained glass, and the general style of decoration is rich and handsome, some of the state-rooms, also, are most sumptuously furnished. Altogether these steamers

---

* The "Isaac Newton" has since been burnt.

are so totally different from anything we have at home, that one who has not seen them can hardly form a correct idea of their appearance, but, like the hotels, they have been described over and over again, and so I will leave them. Next to this is the ferry to Jersey city, at which place is the Cunard dock, occupying the same relative position as that in Boston. Further on is a line of fine boats running to Stonington on Long Island Sound, en route for Boston. These are the finest of the Sound Boats; there are two of them, the "Plymouth Rock" and "Commonwealth." The next Steamship wharf is that of a line running to Aspinwall, on the Isthmus of Panama, and owned by Mr. Vanderbilt. I cannot however say much in favour of them. I have been on board two, the "North Star" and the "Northern Light," and more vile accommodations I never saw—a height of six feet in the state-rooms, and three tiers of berths in each. The ships are pretty fair models, but have a wretchedly dirty, untidy appearance, and the whole management is inconceivably bad. Near this is a line of very good boats running to New Orleans and the Havannah, of these the "Cahauba" and "De Soto" are very fast vessels, and are comfortably fitted up inside. Passing on we come to the wharf of the Galway Steamers, and next to them is a line to Havre and Southampton, consisting of the "Arago" and "Fulton," both very good substantial boats of about 2,200 tons, not fast, but comfortable, well managed, and consequently safe.

A short way above this, and at the foot of Canal Street is the pier originally used by the "Collin's" line of Atlantic Steamers, and now owned by the Company which has bought up the three remaining vessels of the original fleet. This is the last pier at which there is any regular line of vessels, and I wish now to say a few words on the subject of the rivalry existing between us and the Americans with regard to ocean steaming. Although they claim for Fulton the honor of inventing steam navigation (falsely as we know), yet they never attempt to deny that to us belongs the merit of introducing Ocean Steamers. If I remember rightly, their first regular line of Transatlantic steamers ran to Havre, and consisted of the "Washington," "Herman" and "Humbolt," the first of which left New York in 1845, and notwithstanding their boasted superiority, was beaten by two full days by the "Britannia," then one of the Cunard Fleet: and till the establishment of the Collin's line, these steamers were the only ones sailing across the Atlantic under the stars and stripes. The building and starting of the Collin's Steamers was certainly a bold and splendid enterprise, and deserved success; the "Atlantic" the first vessel, being superior in size, model, and internal equipments to the "Asia" or "Africa" than the largest of the Cunard fleet. And for a time they did succeed, but people soon discovered that that great requisite on board a ship at sea, discipline, was totally wanting on the American ships, while it was in a state of highest perfection in the British vessels. Misfortune soon followed in the loss of the "Arctic," and besides the withdrawal of public confidence, they had to suffer from the unwillingness of their own Government to advance them any kind of subsidy. Meantime however the "Baltic" had carried off the laurels, for speed, and remained champion of the sea, the new Cunard Steamer "Arabia," though of equal size, being unable to cope with her in speed. In 1856 the "Persia" appeared, to win back the lost honors of the British Steamers, and started on her first voyage in company with the Collin's Steamer "Pacific." On board the American ship they must have felt that their chance was gone, when they saw this magnificent vessel prepared for the race, the British ship being far superior to the American in point of size and power, and quite equal to her in beauty of form. *But the "Pacific" was doomed never to try her speed

* I was told by the chief officer of the "Persia" that the chief engineer of

with her rival; the "Persia" reached New York after a voyage rendered frightfully dangerous by ice and fogs, and the "Pacific" has never since been heard of. But the enterprise and spirit was not yet crushed out of the New Yorkers, they prepared to surpass the new Cunarder, and in 1858 launched the noble "Adriatic." She exceeded the "Persia" in size by some 300 tons and her lines were certainly finer, but her machinery was at fault, and moreover this last effort had ruined Collins. She made one passage to Liverpool and back, and then the Company expired, after fighting manfully to the last, thus leaving the victory in the hands of our vessels. It is but just, however, to remember that the American Government gave no help whatever to their own line, while Cunard's Company has been for a long time in possession of a large subsidy. Still, a great deal of the bad fortune attending Collins' vessels arose from want of care in the selection of officers and crew, the latter being invariably changed for every voyage, and moreover we must take into consideration the state of perfection to which their rivals had been brought, for I can say, without hesitation, that, in no service, mercantile or otherwise, could eight ships be brought together whose discipline and arrangements are equal to those of the Cunard Fleet.* And the result of this is that whilst other companies have lost numbers of vessels by various kinds of

---

the "Pacific" was on board the "Persia" just before the vessels sailed, and that he, having been "liquoring up" most likely—observed on leaving— "We'll lick you, or go to H——, I guess," little dreaming how prophetic his words were.

* Since the above was written, many changes have taken place. The Cunard Company have added to their fleet the "Australasian" of 2,800 tons and the "China" of 2,560 tons both screw steamers, and lastly the "Scotia," paddle wheel steamer of 4,200 tons. This vessel being the largest merchant vessel afloat except the "Great Eastern."

The "Adriatic" has since been purchased by the Galway Company, and now sails under the British flag. She is registered at 3,600 tons British measurement.

disaster, the Cunard Company, since its first establishment eighteen years ago, has lost but one vessel, the "Columbia," and in that case, not only were all the passengers and crew, with their luggage, and the ship's mails and cargo saved, but even the fittings of the cabins, &c., and the engines. The "Adriatic" and "Atlantic" are now owned by another Company, and are again running across the Atlantic, between New York and Havre. The first-named vessel requiring more than a mere passing notice, I will endeavour to give some idea of her peculiar features. She is without exception the largest wooden vessel afloat, being 350 feet in length, 50 feet broad and 33 feet deep from the main deck. Her saloons are fitted up very beautifully, especially the dining saloon, which occupies a deck house, and is about 70 feet long by 35 feet wide, while below is another long saloon extending nearly the whole length of the ship, and having state-rooms opening off it. The decoration of this room is very showy, but is somewhat cheap and tawdry-looking, whilst the extreme lowness of the roof, only 6 feet 8 inches, and the want of light render it anything but a cheerful-looking apartment. The state-rooms are the same height, and cannot be compared for comfort with those of the Cunarders. Externally the "Adriatic" presents a truly magnificent appearance; her lines are perfection, and she sits on the water more gracefully than any vessel I ever saw, with the single exception of the "Great Eastern." She has the usual American upright stem, and rounded stern, and is rigged with two light masts; which, as well as her two unusually high funnels, rake to a degree I never saw equalled in any large vessel. This fine ship seems to have been started afresh under much better auspices than at her first appearance; she is well officered, and equipped, and is a great favourite with the travelling public.

In several accounts which I have seen given in our papers

of this and other American vessels, I have noticed that their tonnage has been given almost invariably incorrectly, owing to the difference which exists between our method of reckoning and that which is in use in the United States; the American method making a ship more tonnage than our's does. Thus I remember seeing a list of some of the largest steamers afloat; and their tonnage was given, as in the first column:

| | | | |
|---|---|---|---|
| (British meas.) Great Eastern...18,878 tons. | Great Eastern...20,000 tons |
| Adriatic... ... ... 5,879 ,, | Adriatic ... 4,125 ,, |
| Vanderbilt (American) ... 5,300 ,, | Vanderbilt ... 3,350 ,, |
| (British meas.) Persia ... 3,309 ,, | Persia ... 3,680 ,, |

Any one looking at this would imagine the "Adriatic" to be near twice as large as the "Persia," which I need hardly say is very far from being the case. The fact is, that the 5,879 tons of the "Adriatic" are a very great stretch of the imagination; her actual tonnage by American measurement being 4,125, while by ours it is 3,600. Above, I have given the tonnage of the four vessels named, first, as it is generally (and erroneously as regards the two American ships) stated; and secondly, the exact and true measurement of each, according to the American method, and the correctness of which I can vouch for. The fact is, the American measurement is very nearly similar to our own carpenter's or builder's measurement, which, as is well known, gives a vessel more tonnage than does the register. The tonnage of our steamers is moreover still further diminished by their being *officially* registered without the engine-room; for example, on the sea-going certificate on board the "Persia," she is registered at 2,079 tons, the register of the engine-room (1,230 tons) being deducted from her entire tonnage. But I have bored you quite enough with steamers, and will therefore bring this letter to a close. My next shall treat of matters more interesting.

## LETTER X.

NEW YORK.

This letter is to be devoted to Ecclesiastical subjects; for though you and H. may not find it particularly interesting; I know that J. will, more especially as it is ground which has been little touched on in any works I have seen on America. New York is the great strong-hold of the American Church, which here occupies nearly, if not quite as prominent a position, as the Established Church does in London; both numerically and intellectually. But what is of more consequence, it is also the focus of the Catholicity of the church, and presents in this respect a delightful contrast to Boston. Before, however, speaking of the Church as a body, I must try to give you some idea of the different services in the more prominent of the City churches, as well as of the buildings themselves, and shall begin with Trinity. Trinity parish was originally endowed by Queen Anne, and was for a long period the sole parish in New York. It is now by far the most important, not only in the city, but in the country. I cannot define its limits very accurately, for it appears to own ground all over the city, and its wealth is something enormous. The financial and temporal affairs generally, are managed by a committee of vestry-men, having at their head a comptroller; and its spiritual direction is in the hands of a rector and nine or ten assistant clergy. In addition to the parish church, there are three chapels, namely, S. Paul's in Broadway, S. John's in Varrick Street, and Trinity Chapel in 25th Street : and there are also several other churches in the city, which have been built and endowed by Trinity. Trinity Church, as I have already mentioned, is situated at the head of Wall Street in Broadway, and is a large third-pointed building ; consisting of a nave with side aisles, a chancel (also with aisles,) and a tower and spire, at what *ought* to be the west end, though it is in fact the east end. The nave contains seven bays and the chancel, which is the same height and width as the nave, contains two.

The westernmost bay (supposing the church to stand correctly) is occupied on each side by an open porch, and the two bays of the chancel aisle are considerably lower than those of the nave aisles, thus forming the only external indication of the existence of any chancel at all, the chancel clerestory being supported by flying buttresses : the roof is of good pitch and is covered with lead. The aisle and clerestory windows are of three lights each and exhibit the most ordinary form of third-pointed tracery. The tower is very bold and massive and by far the best feature in the building : the *west* front is divided into four stages, the entrance porch occupying the lowest, and a five light window the next, which above come the clock-face, and two large three light belfry windows. The lower stages of the sides are somewhat unsatisfactorily ornamented by empty inches, which don't look as if they were ever meant to contain statues. At each corner of the tower is a bold, and at the same time graceful, pinnacle, from the base of which spring flying buttresses supporting a beautiful crocketed spire. Altogether this tower and spire constitute the best specimen of pointed architecture I have seen here, and indeed would be an ornament to any city. The extreme height of the

spire is 230 feet, and there is a very good stairway to within
40 feet of the top. Inside the tower is a fine peal of 12
bells by Mears of London. The interior of the church is at
first sight really striking, by reason of its great size and the
general church-like character of the design. The piers of
the arches supporting the clerestory are of very good design,
as is also the vaulting of the roof, which however is unfortunately only a plaster imitation of stone. The light is
thrown high, and is subdued by painted glass in all the
windows, not however of very good quality. The chancel is
fitted up with plain oak stalls for the choir and clergy,
and is paved with coloured marble. The altar stands in
front of a somewhat poor-looking reredos, coloured and
gilded, but is not of dimensions suitable for so large a
church, nor is it properly vested—and the ornaments are
all at present wanting; although a pair of handsome candlesticks has been presented, and will I dare say soon appear in their proper place. The altar window is of large
size and consists of seven lights; it is filled with stained glass,
some of the colouring of which is very good, although it
would be far more suitable for architecture of an earlier date.
The organ occupies the interior of the tower, and has a handsome oak front in the church, with the choir organ in a separate case. The projecting balcony in which the organist
sits, as well as the case of the organ, is of exceedingly good
design, and is altogether a really beautiful specimen of wood
carving. The instrument is a very large one by Erben of
New York, and has 16 feet metal speaking pipes in front.
There are services in this church daily, and the doors remain
open all day long. The week-day services are simply read,
but on Sundays and Saints' days there is full choral service,
performed by a regular surpliced choir, and exceedingly well
performed, the boys being admirably trained by Mr. Cutler
the organist, who was formerly organist of the Church of the

Advent in Boston. At Easter and Christmas the decorations in flowers are often very beautiful, and altogether things are done here with decency and in order. The choral service has only been established about a year and a half, and it has already become so popular, that even on Saints' days the church is crowded. The internal dimensions of Trinity are as follows:—

    Length of the nave............... 140 feet.
          of the chancel............ 30 feet.
    Total internal length of Church 170 feet (this does not of course include the Tower.)
    Width of nave...................... 35 feet.
         of aisle........................ 17½ feet each.
    Total width......................... 70 feet.
    Height of nave vaulting.......... 76 feet.

These dimensions are I think nearly correct, but if I err at all, it is in not making the church large enough. S. Paul's Chapel next claims attention. This is situated opposite Barnum's Museum and is the oldest church in the city, the present Trinity having been built in 1845, and being the third church which has been built in the same site. S. Paul's is a Grecian building, and has a tower and spire at the west end, (the real west end I mean, as it has its altar to the east) and a portico at the east end, which faces Broadway. Internally it somewhat resembles (though on a much smaller scale) S. Martin's-in-the-Fields in London, and has the pulpit in the centre right in front of the altar, which however is of good size and made of white marble, with a large corona filled with wax candles hanging in front of it. The body of the church remains much as it was when Washington used to attend service in it, and the pew which he occupied is still pointed out. The organ is an old one built by England, and sent out somewhere about the year 1790: it is a very good instrument. The service is of the regular Protestant type, and the choir a quartette, although the clergy both here, and in all the Trinity Chapels, are men of truly Catholic principles, and will I have no doubt soon bring about a new state of things. There is service only on Sundays and Saint's days except during Lent, at which season there is daily prayer.

S. John's in Varrick Street is a church of much the same style as S. Paul's, but is much larger, and more ornate in its design. It has lately received the addition of a semicircular apse, which is handsomely decorated in colour and gold. The altar is of marble, inlaid in different colours, and ornamented with alabaster: it is never vested, however, and consequently looks very unanglican, though grand and imposing from the extreme richness of its construction. The seats for the clergy are placed stallwise, and are (together with the pulpit, which stands on the left-hand side,) ornamented in gold and colour, while the rich effect of the whole is enhanced by the beautiful marble pavement. Altogether this is by far the best Grecian chancel I ever saw, although it is unfortunately too small to accommodate conveniently a surpliced choir, should the clergy ever succeed in having one: in my sketch I have represented the church as it appeared last Christmas when decorated. The organ stands in the gallery over the door and is a most beautiful instrument, its tone being rich and full beyond almost any modern organ I ever heard, it has the choir organ in front: the services and music are of the same character as at S. Paul's. In connection with the chapel is a Boys' School, from which it is hoped that materials for a choir may be obtained at some future time; and besides this school, there is also an Industrial and Sunday School numbering altogether some 1,200 children.

Trinity Chapel in 25th Street was built some two or three years ago, and is a large first pointed church, consisting of a nave without aisles, and an apsidal chancel. I cannot admire the exterior of the building, the long row of single lancet windows on each side, together with the absence of any tower or spire giving it a monotonous and flat appearance. The front facing 25th Street is the best part of the external design, the door-way being very fine, and there is also a good circular window in the gable. Internally, however, it is very striking, and reflects credit on its architect. The nave, about 130 feet long by 40 broad, is lighted on each side by seven tall lancet windows, which do not reach within twenty feet of the floor, the space beneath them being relieved by an arched recess under each window. The roof is an open oak one of exceedingly good design, the beams are supported on brackets which rest on clustered shafts springing from variably carved corbels between the windows. The chancel, which is about 36 feet long including the apse, is fitted up with oak stalls, the higher row having carved canopies—and here is one of the greatest mistakes in the building, the canopies run right round the apse, of course in many places having no seats under them. The altar stands in the chord of the apse, and, after the Basilican fashion, has the Bishop's seat directly behind it—it is of Caen stone, very elaborately polychromed. The chancel windows are all filled with stained glass, of which however I cannot say I thought much; they are in that "Munich" style which resembles large transparancies far more than stained windows. The roof between the beams is painted of a light blue, powdered with gold stars, and the beams themselves are enriched with colour, which has been used, though too sparingly, and not altogether with good judgment, throughout the church: the clustered shafts supporting the roof, looking unfortunately like barber's poles. The nave is lit at night by handsome gas standards, and the chancel by a beautiful brass corona. The seats of the nave are of oak, and are low and open, (though most of them are appropriated,) and the floor is laid with encaustic tiles, which I believe came from England. On the right hand side of the chancel arch is the pulpit, a very pretty one, with a conical shaped sounding board, which, together with the pulpit itself, is richly polychromed. On the opposite side is the font (a queer position for it truly), of Caen stone and with a handsome cover. The organ occupies a chamber, having two arches, one opening into the chancel, and the other into the nave, but it is quite invisible; it is a large instrument, though somewhat harsh in tone, and awkward to play upon. The choir, consisting of a double quartette, sit on each side of the chancel, and are concealed by abominable red curtains, thus showing that they feel the incongruity of having females as singers in such a place. There is a daily service as at Trinity, but on Sundays only, with music, and then, merely, the singing of the Canticles and Hymns, except in the evening, when the psalms for the day are generally chanted. The interior of the building is lined entirely with white Caen stone, and having a height of seventy feet, it is very church-like and imposing, and certainly no expense was spared in its erection, 280,000 dollars (about 57,000 *l.*) having been spent upon it. Grace Church in Broadway is at first sight an imposing-looking church : it is built of a very light coloured stone, almost white, and consists of a nave and transepts, both with aisles and a very small chancel, with a tower and spire at the west end. The general design is good, and so is some of the detail, (the west door especially), but there is a want of solidity and repose about it, which renders it unsatisfactory. The tower, although its outline is good, is terribly thin and poor in its construction, and the spire is meagre to the last degree. The aisles of the nave project formed level with the front of the tower, so the west front has three large canopied door-ways; over the centre is a Catherine wheel window of pretty design. The style of the church and parsonage which adjoins it, and is very pretty, is second pointed of the flamboyant period. Internally it is I believe very bad, (I never was inside), and the ritual is nil; the clergyman being of extremely Protestant views, and the music of the most splendid operatic nature. A highly fashionable audience attends this church on Sundays, during the colder months; in Summer it is shut up. Calvary Church in 4th Avenue is a large cruciform building of atrocious design (by the same architect as Grace Church), all styles and periods of mediæval architecture being mixed and jumbled up together. S. Thomas' in Broadway is a church of peculiar design, having no aisles or chancel, and a huge broad open wood roof. The effect of its interior is somewhat pleasing (not looking at it in the light of a church), but its exterior is very poor. The most correctly arranged church in the city is the Church of the Holy Innocents in 35th Street. It is a wooden church, and it is hoped merely the fore-runner of a good substantial stone edifice, to be erected at some future period. It consists of a nave, chancel, organ chamber, vestry and porch, and above the east gable of the nave, there is a small bell tower. The chancel is very well arranged with stalls, and there is an oak rood-screen, bearing a large cross. The altar is of good size, and is elevated six steps above the nave; it is correctly vested (there being handsome frontals of each colour), and has a cross and two lights. There is a boy choir and Helmore is used, the services being, as far as is compatible with the limited resources at command, choral, and there is, moreover, weekly celebration of the Holy Eucharist. The chancel roof is beautifully painted in polychrome, the decoration managed in such a way that it can be removed to the new church when it is built. The decorations at Christmas were most beautiful, and amongst other things, consisted of a corona and two enormous standards before the altar, entirely covered with evergreens, and holding about thirty wax candles each, all of which, together with the altar lights, were burning at the *midday* celebration: at least this was the case on Holy Innocents' Day, and I believe, also on Christmas. All the seats are free, and the church was built and is supported entirely by voluntary subscription. I need hardly say that Mr. Elmendorff, the priest, is a truly Catholic and hard-working man; he has also the charge of a Young Ladies' School, conducted somewhat on the same principle as S. Margaret's College at Crieff, in Perthshire. I must not forget to mention a small Missionary Chapel which has been opened on Madison Street, and where an attempt is made at a choral service. It is merely a small room, over a stable, but is very nicely fitted up, and contains a good altar, which is duly vested, and ornamented with a cross and lights. This chapel is the only place in New York; indeed, I imagine, almost the only place in America, where there is a midnight Christmas celebration; but in spite of much praiseworthy efforts, the place is not in good odour, even with the Catholic-minded portion of the community, owing to the line of conduct pursued by its proprietor, for it is in fact a private chapel. The church of the Holy Communion on Sixth Avenue, is a pretty little cruciform church without aisles, and having a tower at the south-west corner of the nave. Internally, its general effect is very pleasing; the seats are all open, and the altar, which is raised five or six steps above the nave, has a huge canopy over it and a large cross painted behind it. Although this arrangement is very peculiar and odd, yet the general effect is good.

There is a boy choir, who are however not surpliced, and daily service is performed with weekly communion. The organ occupies a small gallery in the north transept, and is a nice little instrument: opposite to it, in the south transept, is a very fair circular window filled with pretty good stained glass. There is a Sisterhood in connection with the church, and the priest is a hard-working energetic man, though unfortunately holding and propounding some very peculiar doctrines. I forget to whom the great stronghold of the Low Church party is dedicated, and it does not much signify, as it is always known as Dr. Tyng's church. I never was inside it, but two facts will illustrate the nature of the services: the altar stands in the body of the church, and has a circular railing all round, and 800 dollars (160*l.*) a year are paid for the services of a female singer. None of the Roman churches are such as to merit notice, although a new Cathedral is being built on Fifth Avenue, which will, as far as size and materials are concerned, be very fine. It is being built entirely of white marble, and will be over 300 feet in length, but I fear they have made a mistake in choosing for their architect, the designer of Grace Church, and Calvary. There is one building which struck me very much, and which is in some respect the best ecclesiastical edifice in New York. This is an Unitarian place of worship on Fourth Avenue: it is in the Italian round-arched Gothic style, and is built of red and white bricks, with Caen stone dressings. It is cruciform without aisles, and has a very elegant dome at the intersection of the transepts, composed almost entirely of stained glass. The entrance is through a beautiful triple porch: having polished granite shafts supporting arches profusely decorated with stone carving, while the coloured bricks are arranged in the most pleasing and judicious manner. Over this door is a very handsome circular window, and the gable is crowned by a large and beautiful stone cross. There is to be at one angle, a lofty campanile, but this has not yet been commenced. The interior walls are profusely decorated in fresco and polychrome, and the stained glass is really good. The New Yorkers' taste not being sufficiently cultivated to enable them to appreciate the beauty of this building, they have nicknamed it the church of the Holy Zebra.

There is certainly a considerable difference between the Americans and ourselves in the general tone of church feeling, and one thing is very noticeable, namely, the much greater reverence and attention paid to the Holy Eucharist, by even the Low Church party in America, than by the same portion of the community with us. They attend more frequently, and the Communion Office is invariably accompanied with music, the choir always remaining to sing the Gloria in Excelsis, and the Hymn, which according to the American rubric, is to be sung immediately after the prayers of consecration, oblation and invocation; you will, moreover, see persons, who would leave the church, were the priest to enter the pulpit in a surplice, or were the service intoned, kneeling before an altar of the richest marble, and afterwards joining heartily in the singing of the Gloria. In general, too, they will stand any amount of "preaching to" without taking offence: I heard a very strong sermon on the duty of fasting, &c., in S. John's, where the congregation is decidedly of Low Church inclinations: but they listened most attentively, and I have no doubt many acted upon the admonition. The fact is, the great tide of the Catholic movement has only just reached America, and the devoted energy with which many of the clergy have thrown themselves into the work, cannot fail to produce great and glorious results. There is, of course, the mass yet to be stirred and put in the right way, but the root of evil is not so deep down in the soil, as it was in England: few American churchmen, of whatever party they may call themselves, deny such doctrines, as the Apostolic Succession, and Baptismal Regeneration; moreover, there is not that insane "no popery" feeling to struggle against, at least not to anything like so great an extent as with us. One of the great misfortunes of the American church is her mutilated office book, the state of which most of the clergy deeply deplore. The Communion Office indeed has the prayers of oblation and invocation, and in that particular perhaps may be preferred to the English office, though the prayers are inserted *after* instead of *before* the consecration, therein following the example of the Scottish rite. There are also several useful offices which we lack, such as that for the "Institution of Ministers," (in which by the way the altar is several times *called* an Altar) and also for the consecration of Churches and Burial grounds. Among the mutilations most to be regretted are, the non-insertion of the Athanasian Creed, and of the absolution in the "Visitation of the Sick," as also the omission of the Magnificat, for which and the Nunc Dimittis, are substituted two Psalms. If, however, the rubrics which countenance, and indeed, order ritualism, are omitted, there is on the other hand no rule which can interfere with the highest order of ceremonial, and the priest is equally at liberty to officiate in a dress-coat or the most magnificently embroidered chasuble and alb, or cope. On the whole, the future prospect of this great branch of the Anglican Church is a bright one, and the movement is more likely to succeed from its having commenced in the most influential parish in the country—the example of Trinity Church, is sure to be followed sooner or later. The church is represented in the Press of New York by three papers, nearly answering to the London* "Union," "Guardian" and "Record." The "New York Churchman" and the "Church Journal," representing respectively the "Union" and "Guardian," while the "Record" finds a counterpart in the "Protestant Churchman."

---

* At the time this was written, the *Union* was the sole organ of the so called "Ritualists," who are now represented by half a dozen weekly journal*s*, at the least.

# LETTER XI.

NEW YORK.

JUDGING from some remarks in your last letter, you seem to have conceived some very erroneous ideas on the subject of American society; I shall therefore give you a brief statement of my own impressions on that head. I think the Americans have been hardly dealt with by many writers, though it is true they are themselves partly to blame, for (like Topsy) they make capital of their own shortcomings. People who merely travel in steam-boats, and put up at great hotels, see about as much of American Society, as they would of that of London or Edinburgh, did they spend their whole time, travelling backwards and forwards on a penny Thames Steamer, or on the Portobello Railway. The truth is, that much misrepresentation, or (perhaps I should say) misapprehension, has arisen, from the fact that there are hundreds of people in this country, whose sole claim to the title of "gentleman," is founded on a lavish expenditure of money; but whose language, manners, and general tone of thought and feeling, forbid their being recognized as such, by any really well-bred American. These are the people you generally meet at the hotels, and on the steamers. They spit, and chew tobacco, behave in a disgusting way at table, and display their independence generally; the women, often being as bad as the men, (save in the matter of chewing.) At home we do not come in contact with persons of this class, and are therefore apt to imagine, that this lack of refinement is confined to America, and that it does not exist with us. Republicanism is, (in my opinion) the root of the mischief; for when distinctions of rank are not recognized, men are apt to assume positions for which they are wholly unsuited, and many who might otherwise command esteem and respect, become objects of derision, to those who perceive the incongruity between themselves and their station. There are objectionable people in the best American society, as with us, and no American I ever met, denied this; but to represent their society as totally vulgarized and unintellectual, is very unfair, and only shows that those who do so, have never been in society in the United States. Some of the pleasantest, most lady-like, as well as accomplished women I ever met, were members of old New York families: for, notwithstanding their democratic theory, they are proud; and often justly, of their descent, and keep themselves wholly aloof from the *money* society of the city. *There* indeed, impertinent vulgarity, and coarseness may be seen strutting in all the importance of that pride which has its centre in the pocket. The New Yorkers are, as a rule, most hospitable, and almost kill you with kindness, after having succeeded in making you their guest.*

The ladies, as a rule, dress far more elaborately in the streets than with us, and make up for the excess in that direction by frequently appearing at large evening parties in high dresses and long sleeves, while the gentlemen on such occasions wear frock-coats, quite as often as dress-coats. I have often been amused at the cool impudence of the women

---

* During my residence in New York, I lived, as indeed more than half the people do, in a boarding house: whole families often preferring this most uncomfortable manner of living to the trouble of keeping house.

one sometimes meets in omnibuses and cars, and who, if the car is full, stand and stare you in the face till you give up your seat. I remember a woman getting into a Broadway omnibus, notwithstanding my assurance that it was quite full, and as soon as she had succeeded in squeezing herself in, she handed me in her fare, saying at the same time, "I guess you'd better pay my fare." I did so, smashing my hat against the roof, in the process, and when I turned round, beheld the fair one comfortably ensconced in my seat. But enough of New York for the present. I find that I shall be obliged to start on my visit to Niagara, earlier than I intended. I shall therefore take this letter with me, and finish it there. —— *Niagara.* We left New York on the 15th June, at six in the evening, and by half past seven were passing the "Palisades," a series of basaltic rocks on the west side of the river. Beautiful villas and country houses are scattered over the right bank of the river, to a considerable distance above New York; and the hills on each side, though scarcely meriting the appellation "lofty," are of considerable height and well wooded. The Hudson river railway skirts the shore, throughout its whole distance; and passes through several towns and villages, the names of a few of which I may mention. At the head of Manhattan Island is the town of Spuyton-Devil, beyond it Yonkers, and a little further on Peekskill, Tarrytown, and Poughkeepsie: a little above the last named place, on the opposite shore of the river, is West Point. Here the scenery is truly magnificent, although, (owing to our passing at night) our view was by no means so satisfactory as I could have wished. The hills here, attain a height of 3,000 feet, and rise in bold, rugged precipices almost directly from the river, which winds in amongst them, seeming at times to be lost, until, on turning a lofty promontory, you see it again stretching away before you. I shall never forget my moonlight view of this noble river; I think it looked almost grander than in day-light. A profound stillness, broken only by the monotonous beat of the paddles, or by the rumbling of a passing train, (which looks like a huge glow-worm creeping along the base of the dark mountains overshadowing the water), adds impressiveness to the scene, which would certainly not harmonize so well with the noise and racket, which goes on in these boats during the day-time. I did not retire until 2 o'clock, about which hour we passed Newbourgh, with the Catskill mountains in the distance; and had just got into a sound slumber, when I was awakened by a most appalling noise. My state-room being close to the boilers, I at once conjured up awful visions of an impending explosion, but soon discovered that the noise proceeded from the steam whistle, which was kept blowing at intervals on account of the thick fog which had set in. Sleep was out of the question, and there was nothing for it but to get up again, which I did and went into the saloon, where I found a temporary resting place on one of the sofas. After remaining there for some hours in a miserable condition between sleeping and waking, I was shaken wide awake by one of the stewards, who informed me that we were close to Albany; and I accordingly hurried into my state-room to perform my morning ablutions before appearing in civilized society. We were soon alongside the wharf, and, on landing, I at once engaged a coach and drove to the station of the New York Central Railway. The train for Niagara, not starting till 11, and it then being only 8 o'clock, I adjourned to the Delavan House, an hotel close to the station, there to enjoy a comfortable breakfast. This is a large and handsome hotel, and at that time displayed a peculiarity in employing female waiters at table, though I cannot think that it was an improvement on the ordinary system. These fair damsels, all wore dresses of a similar pattern, and neat little caps and aprons, and were altogether pleasing to look upon, but not very useful as waiters, the enormous hoops which they all wore being a decided hindrance to the freedom and rapidity of their motions. After breakfast we strolled about near the station, until it was time to take our seats, and at 11 punctually we started, having previously paid our fare and marvelled at its smallness: five dollars, about £.1 for a journey of 250 miles, and by an express train; but travelling is cheaper in every way in America than in Europe. As I have already mentioned, the railroad tracks almost always run up the centre of the streets, and in this case the street was a very narrow one; so much so, as to render the position of any ordinary vehicle we might meet or overtake, somewhat unpleasant. It is true the bell is rung continuously, and the speed is not over ten miles an hour, while passing through a street, but still it *looks* very dangerous; and indeed in New York and the larger cities, the locomotives are no longer admitted, but are left outside the town; the train being then divided, and each car drawn separately through the streets by horses: but the great idea here, is that every one should look after himself. Some parts of the country through which we passed were very pretty, though not strikingly beautiful, except at one point, nearly half way to Niagara, where the railway passed through a deep-wooded glen, skirting a clear rocky stream, and where several lovely glimpses were every now and then to be had. At Utica we stopped half an hour for lunch, at least so the conductor told us, though where to get lunch was a problem, difficult of solution; the station being a mere shed, and the only eatables visible being the contents of a little stall, such as you see at the corners of the streets, kept by an old woman. Certainly, they are many degrees behind us in the matter of station accommodation. After passing " Rome," "Syracuse," and a number of other small towns, bearing great names, we reached Rochester at about 6 o'clock. This is now a thriving and populous city, though twenty years ago it was a mere village; it is situated close to the Falls of the Genesee river, the water-power of which it has turned into dollars and cents, with great success. We crossed the river close to the Falls, and had a pretty good view of them: and were they not within fifty miles of the giant cataract, they would doubtless have obtained more notoriety than they now possess. The cascade is indeed very fine, and the fall of water considerable both in quantity and height, but the beauty of the scene is marred by the numerous factories and mills which surround the spot. At Rochester we changed cars for Niagara, where we were due at 9 o'clock. And now, I began to recall all my preconceived notions of the mighty wonder, (whose fame alone has been sufficient to bring many across the wide Atlantic;) and endeavoured to mould them into some definite shape. I even began to listen at every station for the roar, expecting to hear it at least twenty miles off. The last station at which we were to stop was Lockport, seventeen miles from Niagara, and as I made sure of hearing the Falls at this point, I, on nearing the station, put my head out of the window to listen. Instead, however, of receiving any remarkable impression through the medium of my auditory nerves, I was astounded to see at a distance of perhaps a mile a-head, and right on the track, a tremendous fire, and heard most distinctly, instead of the roar of water, the crackling of the flames, which shot upwards in showers of sparks. At this moment the train stopped, and the mystery was soon explained. The Lockport station was in a blaze, and to pass it was impossible, at least so said the conductor. After waiting two hours, and finding the fire gain strength instead of subsiding (a long shed filled with fuel having ignited) they determined to make a rush, and get past, and we fortunately succeeded in leaving the fire in our rear. This was not accomplished without blistering the paint, and cracking some of the windows of the cars, but most thankful we were to find ourselves again in motion, as we had firmly made up our minds to sleep in the cars all night. At about 11 o'clock we reached the Suspension Bridge, two miles below the Falls, and the moment the train stopped, I popped out my head to listen. Not a sound could I hear, and I began to think Niagara must have run dry; but the truth is, that unless the wind be blowing in a favourable direction, the sound is not audible at any very great distance. Having put down those who were bound for the Canada side, we started off again for the village of the Falls, and now I began to keep my eyes on the alert. The night was moonlight, though not very clear, and as we rattled along close to the edge of the ravine through which Niagara flows after its plunge, I could catch stray glimpses through the trees, of a dazzling white mass, right ahead, and could feel the cool spray blown upon my face. Presently we left the bank, and soon stopped in the middle of a smart little town. On emerging from the cars, I was too much engaged with my luggage to listen for the Falls, and getting into an omnibus, we were deposited, in a few seconds, at the Cataract House, where a comfortable supper at once claimed our attention. While engaged in feeding the inner man, we could distinctly hear the sound of rushing waters. This was not the noise of the Falls, however, but of the rapids; the only indications of the near presence of the thundering cataract being a continuous jar and rattle of the windows. On entering my bed-room, I at once opened the window, and to my delight found that it looked over the rapids. Right before me, glistening in the clear moonlight was the rushing, tumbling foaming mass of waters, bounded on the opposite side by the dark woods of Goat Island, and lost to view behind the houses which cluster round the end of the bridge leading to the island, but I knew that although I did not see the fall, I was looking on those very waters which would, ere I could even walk across my room, have plunged into the abyss of the American Fall which lay not 300 yards beyond. Rising above the houses was a thick mist, through which the trees on the Canada side could be dimly seen, and while the roar and dash of the rapids and the deeper boom of the smaller and nearer cataract filled the air, the whole atmosphere, the ground itself, seemed to tremble and vibrate from some other and greater cause— the voice of the Great Horse Shoe Fall, whose position was indicated by clouds of vapour floating upwards, over the trees of Goat Island. I was more impressed, more awestruck I may almost say, with this sound, (though it was not what I expected), than I could have been by the deafening roar and crash, which I had fancied was produced by the Fall. The voice of Niagara is unlike any thing I ever heard; its own beautiful Indian name, which means "Thundering water," conveys in its grand simplicity a more definite idea than could be given by the most elaborate description. As in all probability you will never see Niagara, you may gain some faint notion of the *character* of the sound, though not of its power and vastness, by imagining the noise of the greatest waterfall you ever heard, combined with the notes of 1000 thirty-two feet organ pedal pipes. There is no actual *din;* you can converse in a whisper on the edge of the great fall, but there is a deep voice at which earth and air alike tremble. I remained looking out upon the rapids nearly an hour, and then retired to bed, being obliged first to insert pieces of paper between the window sashes in order to stop the jarring.

## LETTER XII.

NIAGARA.

My last letter concluded with our arrival here, and every day adds to our admiration of its wonders.

Early the following morning I walked down to the bridge, which spans the rapids on the American side of Goat Island, intending to cross over and take my first view of the Falls. I stood on this bridge to watch the waters as they dashed madly forward to their final leap, and quitted it with reluctance, for a grander or more beautiful sight I never saw. To the left, and looking up the river, you see the vast mass of waters tumbling down towards you, as though they would engulph the bridge and sweep it over the fall, indeed its shaking and trembling seems to warrant such a fear, though it is in reality quite secure. Looking down on the other side, the entire mass of foaming and boiling water disappears suddenly at a distance of 300 yards into an abyss from which rises up the white misty cloud I have already mentioned. This is the American Fall. Passing on, I reached a small islet, separated by a narrow channel from Goat Island, and having on it a mill, and a toll house. At the latter I paid the regular fee of 25 cents, (1 shilling) which is levied on every one on his first visit, and entitles him to go and come, afterwards without any charge. Then crossing another small bridge, I found myself on Goat Island.

Before giving you an account of my first view of the Falls, I shall try to convey to you some idea of the geographical features of the locality, in which I trust my rough plan will assist you. The Niagara river, as perhaps you know, commences a few miles below Buffalo, which is situated on Lake Erie, close to the point at which the river leaves it. It is there about half a mile wide, and continues about the same width until near Grand Island, situated about 20 miles from Buffalo, below which point it widens out to near a mile. Just below Grand Island the rapids commence, and flow on in one broad volume until they reach the head of Goat Island, and here they separate, the narrower channel being on the American side, and ending in the American Fall, while the broad expanse of waters on the Canadian side pours over the great "Horse Shoe" or Canadian Fall, fully nine-tenths of the entire volume of water in the river passing over this fall. The course of the river after passing the falls is at right angles to that of the rapids above, and the deep gorge through which it flows is comparatively narrow. The Horse Shoe Fall occupies its upper end, the American Fall pouring over the side, at right angles with the great fall, and directly facing the Canadian side. On the occasion of my first visit I made my way first to the edge of the American Fall. A narrow pathway led through the thick woods to the top of a steep bank, in which steps were cut. Descending these and crossing a light wooden bridge, I found myself on a small islet, named Luna Island, and at the very verge of the Fall. The view down the river is very beautiful, but little of the Fall itself can be seen; while the Horse Shoe Fall is quite invisible. After remaining on Luna Island half an hour or so, I clambered up the steep path again, and walking a few yards along a broad carriage drive, skirting the edge of the precipice, came upon a grassy mound on which were three or four persons, occupying a rough seat and gazing with silent awe and wonder at the scene before them, the most mighty cataract in the world. How can I hope to describe it—who can give any idea of that sea of bright emerald green waves, rolling ceaselessly down into the mist and clouds, which always envelope the base of the fall? There is no rush and plunge, apparently; to me it seemed to roll over more like the waves of the sea, than any waterfall. The water too on the edge of the fall, is intensely green beyond any thing I ever saw, and it is only when about to lose itself in the clouds of mist and vapour which rise up high into the air, that streaks of white become visible, on its surface. This appearance is not observable at the extremity of the fall, for there the water is shallow; it is near the centre of the semicircle, where the depth of water on the edge of the fall is twenty feet, that this vivid green colour appears. But who thinks of feet and inches, and gallons of water and such things when gazing on this stupendous cataract? The water below the fall when it first emerges from the mist, is of a creamy whiteness, and circles round and round in slow eddies, as though stunned by the plunge, gradually however breaking into waves which hurry forward with rapidly increasing velocity until at the suspension bridge, the water is rushing along at a rate of some thirty miles an hour. Near the fall, however, it is comparatively still water; sufficiently so, to permit of boats crossing to the Canada side. A small steamer conveys persons desirous of viewing the fall at close quarters, from the landing at the foot of the American Fall close up to the Horse Shoe. After enjoying the view for some time, I proceeded a short distance further along the drive, to another halting place, from which a path led down to Terrapin Tower, situated on the eastern edge of the Horse Shoe. The tower is built on a rock, round which the boiling waters pour with resistless fury, making tower and rock tremble, and suggesting the strong probability of a sudden descent of both into the abyss. I enjoyed the spectacle from the top of the building as much as was possible in company with five or six exceedingly Yankeefied Yankees, but as I intended to re-visit this spot, did not then stay very long, but returned to the road and continued my walk entirely round Goat Island, passing on my way three pretty little wooded islets close to the shore (of Goat Island), among which the torrent poured in a series of beautiful little cascades. I reached the hotel in time for dinner, at about 2 o'clock ; and was much amused during the progress of the meal by the military manner in which the waiters performed their duties, under the command of the head waiter, a most immaculate swell, though a nigger, and who had drilled his corps to a state of perfect subordination. After dinner I engaged a carriage, and drove over to the Canada side, crossing the suspension bridge. On our way up from the bridge we passed the Clifton House, a fine large hotel, from which there is a beautiful view of both falls. It stands about half a mile below the Horse Shoe, and immediately opposite the American Fall, the whole range of falls extending over nearly four-fifths of a mile. Close to the edge of the Horse Shoe, there is a projecting rock, known as "Table rock" a portion of which has fallen, and the remainder is so cracked as to render its fall a matter of daily expectation. There are here a number of little shops, at which Indian work is sold, and here also those who wish it, are provided with waterproof dresses, in which they can go a short way behind the fall. I contented myself with going down the stairs which are cut in the rocks, and gazing at the Fall from below. This is by far the finest view, and notwithstanding the discomfort, occasioned by the dripping of water from the rocks above, I stood here for nearly an hour. On returning, I had to pass one place where a small cascade was pouring down right into the path, and not caring to be wet through, I made a run to get past when my foot slipped and down I came, and for a moment I feared that I was gone. Fortunately the path was wide at that point, and I sustained no injury, further than a torn coat, and a few slight bruises. On regaining the top, I started off for the American side, and reached my hotel in time for tea. Next day, I spent the whole morning on Goat Island, and in the afternoon went across by the ferry boat to the Canada side. The boats start from the foot of the rocks close to the American Fall, and are reached by an inclined plane, which consists of a tube, (exceedingly "Slantindicular") enclosing a railroad, and a staircase. You pay your fare in a house at the top, and can then, (if you wish) ride down upon a sort of truck, which is let down by ropes; many people, however, dreading the consequences of a breakage, prefer trusting to their own legs. Indeed, if the rope *did* break, nothing could save the occupants of the little car from being shot down into the water, or being dashed to pieces on the rocks, below. Descending by this railway I entered a boat and was ferried over, enjoying on the way a most splendid view of the falls. I spent but a short time on the Canada side and returned the same way. I found the little steamer ready to make her exciting trip up to the Horse Shoe; and accordingly went on board, and donned the waterproof garments necessary for the occasion. But I saw little, for the mist so covered my spectacles, that they became hindrances instead of aids to vision, and the removal of them left me in but a sorry plight for making observations. The little vessel struggled up to within fifty yards of the great Fall, and then turning round shot down the stream with terrific speed, and at length landed us safely at the foot of the stairs.

At night I went out to see Niagara by moonlight. The moon did not rise till past 10, and it was therefore nearly 11 before I went on Goat Island; there were, however, several parties bent on the same errand. I found that moonlight greatly enhanced the beauty of the scene, and was specially delighted with a lovely lunar rainbow, which was visible through the mist and vapour which rose from the American Fall; (the position of the Horse Shoe Fall being unfavourable for the observance of one there.) On the following day I drove to General Brock's Monument, and visited the whirlpool. Our drive lay through a well-wooded county, and ran along the edge of the Niagara gorge. The whirlpool is about three miles below the suspension bridge, and is visited, not so much for its own sake, as for the grandeur of the deep wooded glen through which the river rushes. There are walks, and stairs cut through the rocks, so that the descent to the water's edge is easy, and the grandeur of the scene well re-pays a visit. After a pleasant drive of eight miles, we suddenly emerged from the woods and found ourselves on the summit of a long chain of hills, while before us stretched a level plan bounded by the vast expense of Lake Ontario. On the left lay the outlet of the Niagara gorge, from which issued the now calm, and unruffled waters of the river, winding through the plain to the ocean-like Ontario; while clustered on its opposite banks lay the towns of Lewiston, and Queenstown, to the former of which we now descended. After taking luncheon, at a somewhat primitive hotel, we ascended the river and crossed it by means of a very pretty suspension bridge, just at the entrance of the gorge, and in a few minutes entered the grounds which surround the monument. The structure consists of a Corinthian column, with a statue on the top, and is quite new, having only lately replaced the original monument, which was destroyed by some ill conditioned individual of Guy Fawkes tendencies. The view from the top is very fine, and extends for many miles over a beautifully wooded country, and far out on the vast blue surface of Ontario. Looking towards Niagara, the position of the Falls was pointed out by the white cloud of vapour rising high into the air, and on listening I distinctly heard their sound, the wind being in a favourable direction. We returned to our hotel by the road on the Canadian side, and crossed the river, at the upper suspension bridge. On the Monday following I made an expedition to Buffalo, a railway ride of twenty-two miles. This city is one of the most extraordinary instances of the rapid growth of American towns with which I am acquainted : the population in 1830 was about 12,000, and now it is nearly 120,000. The town is very well built, the principal thoroughfare, Main Street, being a wide and handsome street, and ascending with a gentle rise from the wharfs, which line the shore of Lake Erie. My stay in Buffalo being limited to a few hours, I was unable to hunt up any of the Anglican Churches, of which there are several, and was obliged to content myself with a survey of the Roman Cathedral. This is decidedly one of the best churches I saw in my tour; it is built of dark gray stone, in the early second pointed style, and consists of nave, transepts and small chancel, all with aisles. The roofs are of open timber, and are adorned with polychrome. There is a great deal of stained glass, and some of it is very fair, though the style of drawing and colouring is not very correct. I succeeded in obtaining permission to try the organ, and having been told that it was built in Buffalo by an almost self-taught workman, was amazed to find a very large, and fine toned instrument, equalling indeed in both respects many organs by first-rate English builders. Before leaving for Niagara, I took a stroll along the wharfs and went on board one of the Lake Steamers, the "Western Metropolis" was (I think) her name, and in beauty of model and internal decorations, she surpassed any of the American Steamers I had seen. The saloon was fitted up with perfect taste, and contained a handsome piano, while pier glasses and marble slabs, (having on them vases full of flowers,) were scattered about in profusion. On the lower deck, just opposite the entrance gangway, there was a marble basin filled with gold fish, and with a pretty little fountain playing in the centre. The docks presented quite a busy scene, and contained numbers of sailing vessels of all sizes, as well as a great many large screw steamers. While at tea in the evening, (after my return to Niagara), I witnessed a sample of the highly polished manners which characterize many of the people one meets at these hotels. The offender was a very pretty girl, whose appearance was decidedly lady-like, till she began her assault upon the viands—and then ensued, such cramming and stuffing! such a display of sword exercise! I trembled for her mouth, fully expecting to see it desperately wounded by the continuous dives which her knife made into its recesses. The said knife was too much occupied, in shovelling up the contents of her plate, to be spared for any operations on the bread, a large slice of which was vigorously assaulted by her teeth, and a huge semi-circular bite taken right out of the centre.

## LETTER XIII.

NEW YORK.

You will be surprised to see from my date, that I have returned hither so soon; but I was obliged to curtail my Canadian tour, and as my time was limited, and I wished to see as much as possible, I really had not leisure to write to you. To make amends, however, for my silence, I shall now give you an account of my proceedings since I left Niagara. I should have been glad to have remained there much longer, for I was never tired of watching its ever changing aspects, or of listening to its ceaseless roar. We started on the 22nd of June, by train for Lake Ontario. I had taken through tickets, which carried us by train to Lewiston, thence by steamer to Montreal, and thence by way of Lakes Champlain and George to Saratoga. I forget what was the exact price of the tickets, but I know it was exceedingly moderate. The railway from Niagara to Lewiston, is carried along the extreme verge of the precipice, the cars seeming at times almost to overhang the torrent, which, 200 feet below, rushes foaming along at a speed greater than that of the train. It certainly looks dangerous, and once or twice loose stones and gravel, shaken by the motion of the train, from underneath the sleepers, went rolling down the bank into the river. I must confess I was glad when our train reached its destination, and we stood on the deck of the "Ontario" steamer; a large vessel, similar to the one I had seen at Buffalo, though not so richly decorated. I procured a comfortable state room, near the stern, and at 3 o'clock afternoon we started, and after steaming about four miles down the Niagara river, the wooded shores on each side abruptly receded, and we were on Lake Ontario. As there was nothing to attract notice on shore, seeing that it was almost out of sight on the American side, and of course far below the horizon on the Canadian, we were glad to find our boat a most comfortable one, and our company agreeable. There was a capital piano in the saloon, and in the evening we had music. About mid-night we reached Oswego, a small town on the American side, and lay there till morning, my slumbers coming to an end in time only to allow me to see the light-house at the entrance of the harbour, as we rapidly steamed away. Towards the afternoon the land became visible on both sides, and soon we saw before us on the left the bright tin covered roofs and domes of Kingston. I was very much struck with the appearance of the town, the bright tin which is used in most Canadian towns to cover the roofs and domes of the public buildings giving a very lively and peculiar aspect to the whole city. The place, however, seemed very deserted, but few people were on the wharfs, when we stopped, and the number of half-finished buildings bespoke a great need of the infusion of a little Yankee-go-ahead spirit. Kingston stands at the entrance of the S. Lawrence, and soon after passing it we came to that part of the river, known as the "Lake of the Thousand Islands." I had been so stupid as to expect hills and rocks, and grandeur generally, in the far-famed S. Lawrence, and I am afraid I did not rightly appreciate the softer though undeniable beauties of the Thousand Islands. Late in the evening we reached Ogdensburg, where we we to remain till morning, to be then transferred to a smaller steamer, in which to descend the rapids. This was, to me, by far the most interesting part of our voyage, and is altogether quite an exciting affair. Having been duly transferred bag and baggage into the other boat, we started at 9 o'clock, and in about an hour reached the first and by far the mildest rapid. Indeed the only indications of the existence of a rapid were the short waves which covered the surface of the water, and a few patches of white foam : the steam, however, was shut off and we were carried down by the current. This was quite a short rapid, and I began again to feel disappointment, until we entered the "Long Sault" rapids. Here we were carried along at a tremendous rate, the water foaming and lashing against the side of the vessel, making her reel over every now and then. After passing the "Long Sault," there came an interval of quiet waters, and then a long line of foam, and breakers a-head announced our approach to the "Cascade Rapid." This though not extending above a mile in length, (whereas "Long Sault" is above ten miles long) is a still fiercer rapid than its predecessor, and the bow of the boat seemed sometimes about to plunge right under water, whilst clouds of spray dashed over the vessel. Beyond this the river expands into a lake about ten or twelve miles long and four or five broad, and after passing through this, we soon came within sight of the last and most dangerous rapid, that of Lachine. The river here is fully a mile broad, but only one little passage exists through which the steamers can pass; the channel not being above 150 feet wide, and hemmed in on each side by a flat topped rock rising some half dozen feet above the surface, and over which the waves foam in breakers, while between them the torrent rushes with fearful velocity. The most delicate steering is required at this point, and the boat bore down at a tremendous speed with her bow pointing directly into one of the rocks, till when within twenty or thirty feet, the current caught her and with a heavy lurch she surged through the narrow opening, just grazing the rocks at either side as she passed. Having recovered from the state of excitement produced by this dangerous bit of navigation, we observed, at a distance of a few miles a-head, what looked like a series of huge stepping stones stretching across the river, two or three couples of them being joined by long black objects—this was the unfinished Victoria Bridge, and beyond it appeared the domes and spires of Montreal, behind which rose up a low flat topped hill. In the course of half an hour we reached the bridge, and passing under the central span, on which the tube was already placed, we quickly arrived at our wharf. Montreal looks exceedingly well from the river, and is a refreshing change after the sameness which characterizes the greater number of American cities, resembling, as it does, an European continental town. This idea is favoured moreover by the predominance of the French Roman Cathedral, a huge building with two square towers, which, although of abominable design, from its great size and the cathedral-like character given by its lofty towers, is a decided ornament in a distinct view of the city. Tin roofs and domes abound as at Kingston, and so, I found on landing, did mud. Such a vile road as that along which we drove to our hotel was never seen. Everything here betokens a very odd mixture of French and English; some of the streets having French, and some, English names written up, while others have both. In the evening I walked out, and went towards the French Cathedral, situated at one side of an open square. The street in which the hotel was, reminded me somewhat of Aberdeen, the stone employed being of a grey colour, very much like granite. The Cathedral was closed, so, after deciding in my own mind that it was one of the ugliest of buildings, I strolled along Notre Dame Street, passing a large and rather handsome public building on the left, opposite to which was an open space extending down to the water. In the middle of this stood a miserable dilapidated column, apparently a monument to some one, whose memory has not continued to claim respect or admiration from the people of Montreal; on enquiry, I was sorry to find that the thing was intended as a monument to Nelson! The following day I joined a party of Americans, (whose acquaintance I had made on board the "Ontario,") in a drive round the "Mountain," as they call the hill behind the city. The view from parts of the road was very pretty, especially that towards the city : on our way we passed a sad record of one of the dreadful fires by which the town has been of late so frequently devasted, the ruins of a fine large Roman Church, S. Jacque's. It was only just finished, and the fire was occasioned by an accident happening to the Sanctuary Lamp, the altar and all its costly fittings and vestments being totally destroyed. The Anglican Cathedral had not long before met with a similar fate, though the circumstance is hardly to be regretted, as the building which was very poor, is now replaced by one of the best churches on the American continent. I was unfortunately not able to procure access to the interior, but its exterior gave promise of considerable beauty, and although of comparatively small size, the general effect was imposing and church-like.

The next day (Sunday) being within the octave of Corpus Christi, there was a grand ecclesiastical procession through the principal streets, and being desirous of seeing the interior of the Cathedral, as well as of witnessing the ceremony, I went to the church and found the procession forming in the interior. There were several sisterhoods present from the different convents, and many others were expected to join at different points, while quite a number of clergy were making preparations. Mass was over when I entered the church, and I therefore had an opportunity of examining the building, which was the most glaring sham I ever set eyes on. Sham wooden pillars painted to represent stone, supported a sham vaulting, while two tiers of galleries ran round three sides. The altar was however fine and free from tawdriness, and above it was a large stained window. Presently I was dreadfully startled by the sudden striking up by a brass band, in the church, of a most secular sounding melody, I am almost sure, a polka, while at the same time the organist commenced playing a totally different tune, on the full organ, the discord being brought to a climax by the sound of a second brass band outside, and the tolling of the great bell. Amidst this horrid din, the procession moved off, every token of respect being paid by those in the streets as the Host was carried along under a splendid canopy. In the course of the afternoon I wandered down to the wharfs, or rather stone quays which extend for a considerable distance along the river, and while prowling about here, my fondness for steam shipping tempted me to go on board the* "Anglo-Saxon," a fine screw steamer running between Montreal and Liverpool. While engaged in exploring the recesses of the vessel, I had not observed the change which had taken place in the weather, and was extremely surprised on coming on deck, for the purpose of going ashore, to find a storm of hail descending, which kept me prisoner for an hour, and prevented me from carrying out my intention of attending afternoon service at the temporary Anglican Cathedral. My position was rendered doubly pleasant by the sitting down to dinner in the saloon of all the officers of the ship, who evidently regarded me as an unwelcome intruder, till at last I was compelled to make a rush, although the rain was by no means over, and succeeded in gaining the hotel, in a soaked condition.

There are many convents in this city; I visited one, and was much pleased with the order and neatness of everything,

---

* Since lost with all on board.

their chapel was a pretty little building, and fitted up with very good taste. During the winter months the river is frozen over, and I should think Montreal must be dreadfully dull. In the spring, the thaw causes the ice to descend in immense masses, great blocks being sometimes piled up along the quays as high as the houses. This has been also the great difficulty in building the Victoria Bridge, which is now however nearly finished and as strong as human hands can hope to make it. The next day we left Montreal, being conveyed across the river in a steam ferry boat to the train which awaited us on the opposite side.

We reached Rouse's Point, at the head of Lake Champlain, in a couple of hours, and after a mere pretence by the official of examining our baggage, found ourselves on board the steamer, and once more under the Stars and Stripes. The country all round Lake Champlain is very picturesque and beautiful, but the lake is too wide at its upper end to enable those on the boats to get a good view of either side, but towards the lower end it narrows to a breadth of one or two miles; and at Fort Ticonderoga, (where we disembarked,) the scenery is exceedingly fine, reminding me very much of parts of Scotland. After scrambling up a steep bank from the landing place, we found three stages, of the abominable construction which prevails all over the country, waiting to convey our party (some thirty in all) across to the head of Lake George. It took us nearly an hour to get packed in like herrings in a cask, and at last we set off, every jolt causing the ten passengers whom our vehicle contained to sway about in one solid helpless heap. Oh the discomfort of these horrid "leathern conveniences," the celebrated "Hawes Fly" must have been a model of speed and comfort compared to them. We took an hour to perform the distance, which was barely five miles, and as I was so unfortunate as to be wedged in between two ladies, I caught only a few intermittent glimpses

of the country. I was very much pleased with the scenery
of Lake George, I believe it is considered the prettiest of all
the American lakes, and reminded me, in some parts, of Loch
Katrine, the size of the two lakes being moreover nearly the
same. But I felt a decided satisfaction in being able con-
scientiously to declare that it could not compare with Loch
Lomond, the queen of our Scottish lakes. Lake George, or
to give it its old Indian name, Lake Horicon, was the scene
of the massacre of British troops by the Indians, in the war
with the French in 1755, and the hotel to which our whole
party was bound, is built on the site, then occupied by Fort
William Henry. The spot is rendered interesting to novel
readers, as being the scene of the events detailed in Cooper's
most delightful work, the "Last of the Mohicans." We
found quite a large party stopping at the hotel, which, although
in such a thinly peopled locality, is in its size and appoint-
ments equal to many in the large cities : its business being
however entirely confined to the summer months. Situated
but thirty miles from Saratoga, the great watering place, it
is a very favourite resort for those who are condemned to
undergo the double process of drinking the waters and
enduring the stifling heat for which that American Spa is
celebrated ; the neighbourhood of Lake George, though hot
*enough*, being perfectly polar in its temperature in comparison.
We remained one night at the Fort William Henry Hotel,
and on the following day took stages for the "Moran"
station, there to take the cars for Saratoga. I was delighted
to find that our conveyance was not the detested form of
vehicle with which I had already made such intimate acquaintance, but a sort of char-a-banc, and very comfortable. The
road too was smooth, being what is called a " plank road," a
name which explains itself; and as we had the additional
advantage of very pleasant companions, our drive of twelve
miles formed a great contrast to the miseries of our ride the

day before. We had to wait an hour at the station, which, although but a shed, could, we were glad to find, boast of a "bar," whereat Sherry Cobblers, &c. were in great request. At last the train arrived, and we started off at great speed along a railroad considered bad even in America. The only thing that saved us from being jolted to pieces was the admirable construction of the cars. As it was: the bumps and jolts with which the wheels met, imparted to the body of the car a jumping motion, which caused the occupants to perform a series of bobbings up and down, similar to the performance of an indifferent equestrian on a rough trotting horse. We reached Saratoga by 6 that evening, and I accompanied a very pleasant family whose acquaintance I had made at Montreal, to the United States Hotel. The town, I thought decidedly pretty, it seems almost made up of hotels, and trees; with pretty gardens nicely laid out, surrounding the different well-houses. I noticed that the ladies, here, all eschew the use of bonnets, and walk about with only a parasol, and often in low dresses. The next day is in my recollection, a blank, my memory retaining only a vague, hazy remembrance of intense, insufferable heat, made worse by my insane efforts to cool myself by fanning and sprinkling of Eau-de-colgne. To *do* any thing was out of the question, one's only care was to find a shady place, (a *cool* place there was not) and stick to it —even those accustomed to American heat, acknowledged that they were overpowered that day.

In the evening, when the heat was less stifling, I accompanied one of our lady travelling acquaintances, in a walk through some of the grounds attached to the Congress Spring, trying a glass of the water, which is about as nasty as most mineral waters are. In the course of our ramble we came upon a circular railway with a kind of velocipede running on it for the amusement of those whose tastes inclined that way. What possessed us I cannot think, but by a simultaneous impulse we proposed a circuitous journey on this affair, and accordingly we proceeded to drive round in an insane manner, and my disgust was not small when on regaining terra firma, and my senses, I found that the heat of the morning had returned with double intensity and that the man in charge of the infernal machine demanded half a dollar. I gave him a two-dollar bill and my sincere blessing (the latter being divided between him and his instrument of torment) and received a bad bill in exchange; a fact which I mention, as it was the only bad money that ever fell into my hands, in a country notorious for the circulation of worthless notes. There is a pretty little lake, about four miles from the town, but I could not go to see it—it was too hot to see anything, or feel anything but stifling oppression by day, and musquitoes at night—though I escaped the latter, wonderfully, when every one else was being devoured.

The following day we reached Albany (a distance of 30 miles), by the same detestable railroad on which we had previously travelled: passing through Troy, a city equalling Albany in size, and distant from it only about ten miles. I went again to the Delavan House, and remained in the town all the following day. Albany being the capital of the State of New York, contains one or two handsome public buildings, and though the town itself is not particularly well built, yet, from its commanding position, (on a slight eminence overlooking the Hudson) its general aspect is pleasing, especially when seen from the opposite side of the river. The principal street runs up from the river to the top of the hill, on which stands the State-house, or Capitol, (I forgot which they call it,) and is very broad, too much so indeed. At the time I was there, a new Anglican Church S. Peter's, was in course of erection, and it promised well: consisting, as far as I could see in its unfinished state, of a nave and chancel with aisles, and a corner tower, in the second pointed style. The only other Anglican Church I saw was St. Paul's, a very ugly Grecian building, decently fitted up and containing a good organ. The chief ornaments of the town, however, are two large Roman Churches, the Cathedral and S. Joseph's.

They are both about the same size, S. Joseph's being perhaps the larger, and certainly, the finer. The Cathedral consists of nave, transepts, and chancel; all with aisles. It has two western towers and is built externally of dark red stone, and in late second pointed. Unfortunately the interior is very *plastery*, both columns and roof being sham, although of good design; the stained glass is abundant and pretty good, and there is a fine large organ in the west gallery, by Erben of New York.

S. Joseph's differs from the Cathedral, in plan, in having one western tower, at the extremity of the nave, and also two lofty turrets, one at each angle formed by the chancel and transepts. The style is early second pointed, and the material, dark slate-coloured stone with white stone dressings, the features most deserving notice being the western doorway which, with the two porches, is very good. Internally the effect of the whole is exceedingly fine, the roof being of open timber, richly carved and polychromed, while the piers of the arches supporting the clerestory are of polished white marble, the capitals being judiciously gilded and coloured. The chancel is apsidal, and has no windows in the walls; the light being admitted through an opening in the roof, and falling directly on the altar. This latter stands in the chord of the apse, and together with its beautiful reredos, is of pure white marble, most richly carved. It is by far the best Roman Altar I ever saw; and the two altars of S. Mary and S. Joseph were in equally good taste; the latter being almost Protestant in its simplicity, and displaying neither cross nor light, but a large Bible. The windows are all filled with stained glass, and some of it is exceedingly good; but the great glory of the Church, is the supurb organ, the largest on the American Continent.

It was built by Simmons and Wilcox of Boston, and contains seventy stops. It stands at the west end of the nave. Having an introduction from a friend in New York, I went to see the studio of Mr. Palmer, an American, indeed I might almost say *the* American Sculptor. One beautiful figure just completed, struck me as being far superior to the Greek Slave, about which every one raved in 1851, and proved that America is not so much benighted in matters of art as is often supposed. You will say to yourself on reading this, that my estimate of the comparative merits of the two pieces of sculpture, is worth nothing; as, a boy of fourteen, as I was in 1851, is incapable of forming a judgment on such points; but I must remind you that I have seen the " Greek Slave" since then.

From Albany, I took the cars direct to Boston, passing through the lovely scenery of the Connecticut valley, by way of Springfield; at which point the railway crosses the Connecticut river, by a long wooden viaduct roofed over, as are all such structures in America. And very provoking these coverings are, for often when looking out on the surrounding landscape, I have seen a river a-head, and have thought " what a lovely view we shall have from the bridge ;" but alas! when the bridge is reached, a horrid din in the ears, and profound darkness before the eyes, are hardly to be regarded as compensation, for the lost view. From Springfield two lines branch off, one going by way of Newhaven to New York, the other, which was my line, to Boston. In Boston I remained three days, and then returned hither; and I do not think I shall leave New York again, until I leave it finally on my return to England. While in Boston, I experienced all the delights of a 4th of July celebration.

On these occasions every one seems beseized with a sudden mania for gunpowder. Pistols, crackers and even guns, (I don't mean field pieces) being fired off promiscuously without let or hindrance, even in the most crowded streets, though as far as I am aware, without any injury being done to life or property.

## LETTER XIV.

NEW YORK.

As I have nothing particular to write about to-day, it occurs to me that I cannot do better, than answer as fully as possible the long list of questions you have put to me, regarding the progress of organ building, and organ playing in America. This letter therefore will be so completely *organic*, that any one who is *not* musically inclined, had better not attempt to read it. To begin then with the builders. The names to be found on the principal organs, in the United States, are, Erben, Jardine, and Robjohn of New York; Simmons and Wilcox, Hook, and Appleton, of Boston. The organ of Trinity Church, New York, is perhaps the best, as it certainly is the largest of Erben's. The compass of each key-board is from CCC. to f$^a$ in alt. the great organ running throughout, the choir to CC., with the lower octave acting on swell bass; and the swell to tenor C., with a sixteen foot Dulciana and reed, on the two bass octaves. The great organ contains two open diapasons throughout in metal; seven ranks of mixture and two reeds, twelve stops in all. The swell contains nine stops, and the choir, eight. There is a thirty-two foot open stop of gigantic size on the pedals; so large indeed, that the three lower notes can hardly be made to speak; but the pipes that do sound, are remarkably fine. The swell is inclosed in a very thick box, with three sets of shutters, which open in succession; and the crescendo effect is in consequence greater than in any other organ I have heard. The tone of the instrument is good, though somewhat deficient in brilliance and power, the diapasons especially being very weak. On the whole, however, it is a fine instrument, and the church being well adapted for music, sounds well. Another of Erben's organs is that in the Roman Catholic Cathedral at Albany, it is a large instrument of much the same character as Trinity, except that its great organ only descends to CC., and the pedal organ has no thirty-two foot stop. As I could not obtain access to this organ, I cannot give any detailed account of it. A number of other instruments by the same maker, are to be met with in different parts of the country all characterized by much the same merits and defects, the two organs which I have mentioned being perhaps the most important. Of Jardine's instruments I have seen but three, (one of which was in his factory,) and I cannot say that I admired them; the tone seemed like that of an exaggerated harmonium. The third named builder, Robjohn, though doing but a very small business, has turned out some of the best instruments in the country, though being an Englishman himself, and employing English workmen, his instruments can hardly be cited as examples of American manufacture. His two largest organs are, one at Troy, a most splendid instrument, with a CC. swell, of 13 stops, an 8 stop pedal organ, and upwards of 30 sounding stops in all; and an equally large and fine one in a 'Dutch Reformed' Church in Fifth Avenue, New York. Both these instruments are finished in the most perfect manner, and their tone is full and brilliant, equalling any modern English organs I ever heard; they are also supplied with pneumatic action. Although a much smaller instrument, the organ of S. John's Chapel, New York, by this builder, is perhaps even more remarkable for its extreme fullness and brightness of tone. Its great organ consists of but eight stops, having six ranks of mixture and one reed, but its tone is magnificent, the open diapason being sonorous and smooth, and the chorus ringing and brilliant. It has a small but sweet toned swell, and a choir organ in front, with two sixteen foot stops on the pedal, a large one of wood and a smaller one of metal, both very effective.

As far as I have seen, I should decidedly give the first place, among American organ builders, to Messrs. Simmons and Wilcox of Boston. Mr. Simmons having a thoroughly practical knowledge of the mechanical details of his profession, and Mr. Wilcox conbining with a great degree of the same proficiency, a most perfect theoretical and practical acquaintance with music. He not only helps to make organs as well as any one I know of, but he also makes them speak afterwards, in a manner I never heard surpassed; the result of the combined action of the two partners being the production of a class of instruments which rival any produced in England. I have not space to describe half the splendid organs of their building which I have seen, and will confine myself to a slight notice of the two which are I believe the finest. The organ of S. Joseph's Church at Albany is, as I have said, the largest ever built on the American continent, and contains nearly sixty sounding stops. The swell runs throughout (as do *all* the swells made by these builders) and contains four reed stops, the great organ contains sixteen stops, and amongst them a sixteen foot double open diapason in metal, ten ranks of mixture and two reed stops, as well as a beautifully toned gamba. The pedal organ contains ten stops, one of them a "a thirty-two foot open." The general tone of the organ is remarkably fine, the reeds and gambas especially, and it is of tremendous power. The other organ of which I wish to speak, is that of Harvard College Chapel at Cambridge, near Boston. Though not so large as the

Albany one, it is I think even better toned, being more delicately voiced; the metal of the pipes too is better, the front open diapason being of pure tin. It has forty sounding stops, including seven on the pedal organ. Some of the solo stops on the choir organ are very beautiful, especially the vox-angelica and the vox-humana, which latter is better than any I ever heard excepting those in the Dutch organs.

The organs of "Hook" of Boston, I cannot admire; their reed and solo stops are very good, and so are their pedal basses, but the great organ is thin and poor. The best of their instruments I saw was that in S. Paul's Church, Boston; but even in this the diapasons of the great organ though sweet were very weak, and the mixtures miserable. The large organ in the Tremont Temple is one of their's, and contains some good points. The swell for instance is very fine, running throughout and containing I think, fifteen stops; the pedal organ also is good: but the great organ, though containing ten ranks of mixture, is wretched—and not a bit more powerful than the swell. This instrument is I believe the only one in America which has a solo organ, though this solitary example is not a very favourable specimen. Appleton has been dead some years, but many of his organs are to be met with, and they are in many respects, good instruments, containing generally but few fancy stops, and but poor reeds, their diapasons and mixtures being, however, for the most part full, and somewhat brilliant. The price of organs in America is, I think, decidedly below the average in England; for example, the great Albany organ cost only 7,000 dollars, or about 1500*l.* and the Harvard Chapel one, 6,000 dollars. It is true, that in such cases, either the work must be inferior, or else the builders must lose, and in the two instances I have quoted, the latter, I know to have been the case. But enough of organs. (By the bye I have always forgotten to answer a question of yours, viz., where is

Brooklyn, and is it a district or a town?) I have seen, in many journals of travels in America, Brooklyn described as a suburb of New York—wouldn't the Brooklynites be savage if they heard their city so insulted. I believe they rather look upon New York as a suburb of Brooklyn. The city is laid out on the same rectangular plan as New York, its two principal avenues running up at right angles with the East River or Sound, "Atlantic Street" being the name of that to the west, and "Fulton Avenue," of the other. These are crossed at right angles by Court Street, and further up by Flatbush Avenue. There are three ferries from New York to Brooklyn, besides others further up the North River, to Green Point and Williamsburgh. These three are the South Ferry between the Battery, and foot of Atlantic Street, Wall Street Ferry, and Fulton Ferry, which last connects Fulton Street, New York, with Fulton Avenue, Brooklyn. The progress of improvement has been much hindered in Atlantic Street, by the custom of driving locomotives through the street, which is still caried on here. It is the more inconvenient, as horse cars run on the same rails with the locomotive trains, which have to keep a sharp look out to avoid running over them. There is also a railroad in Fulton Avenue, but only for horse cars, and I believe that soon the locomotives will be obliged to stop short of the city, and will thus relieve the inhabitants of Atlantic Street from a great annoyance. The City Hall of Brooklyn, stands at the junction of Court Street with Fulton Avenue, and is a fine building of white marble, greatly superior to the New York Hall. A large opera House is also in course of erection here, though whether, in such close proximity to New York, it will pay, is a question. There are some pretty good churches, but no attempt at a choral service. Trinity Church is a large building in very questionable second pointed, but it will have (when completed) a good tower, and has already a fine doorway. Greenwood cemetery is I believe beautiful, but I am ashamed to say I have never been there, always meaning to go "some other day." To a stranger walking along the streets of New York or Brooklyn, New York especially, the question would be very likely to arise, Does this people live on oysters and lager beer. In some parts of the city almost every other shop is an "Oyster Saloon," and they eat them all the year round. One writer in America described their oysters as being not quite so large as a small leg of Welsh mutton, but thought the flavour inferior to ours, I confess I prefer them, although they are so huge—their flavour seemed to me exceedingly pleasant and delicate. What is lager beer? I should answer, the best thing in the world to produce a splitting headache. The first time I ever tasted it, was just before entering an omnibus. I took one glass—on my honour, but one glass—and fell into a oblivious state on the seat of my vehicle, from which I awoke to find myself on the floor, by a great mercy, not in middle of the road. The opening of oysters is quite a trade, and I have often seen advertisements in the *Herald* for a man or boy thoroughly competent to open oysters. The "Great Eastern" is expected to arrive here, the week after next, and as my present intention is to return home in her, you may expect to see me before the end of August. I shall of course write again, before I leave.

## LETTER XV.

The New Yorkers are certainly the most excitable people under the sun: if they can once succeed in making a lion of any person or thing, the object of their admiration or interest is, for the time worshipped, and when their enthusiasm has worn itself out, is often neglected, and even abused. During the spring and summer of 1860 there have been perhaps more causes for this excitement, than have occurred in a single year for a long time past. First, the whole city was in a ferment about the Sayers and Heenan contest, then we had the Japanese embassy, then the "Great Eastern," and the visit of the Prince of Wales, to which they are now looking forward, will I fancy be the culminating point of their excitement, that is to say, unless the threatened troubles in the South do not give them even more cause for a sensation. How I pitied those poor Japanese ambassadors, dragged round the city as they were, for a show and spectacle; they bore it all very patiently, and seemed quite resigned to their fate. They were soon tired of their American tour—railway travelling made their celestial heads ache, and I suspect the rudeness and familiarity to which they were exposed, troubled them more. One of the suite, a saucy boy of sixteen, made great havoc among the hearts of the ladies—but stop, I must, in charity, say no more of that. How thousands of generally sensible American women must blush *now*, on recollecting what egregious fools they made of themselves during the visit of "Tommy." "Tommy," I have no doubt thought it fine fun, when the crowd allowed the carriages of the chief ambassadors to pass with a stare, and saluted *him* with shouts and cheers. He certainly received his ovations in the most dignified manner, as he sat perched on the great wagon which bore the "treaty box," waving his handkerchief and smiling blandly at the ladies. For the credit of New York, however, I must say that it was at Washington and other places that the greatest amount of this foolery was gone through; indeed by the time the embassy reached the Empire city, the excitement was already dying out, and people were beginning to look for the next performance—the arrival of the Mammoth of the Seas.

Ever since the first building of the great ship, I have been one of her most sincere well wishers—and my faith in her success has all along been great. Plenty of persons will always be found to croak and prophesy ill of great enterprises, and I think the Great Eastern has suffered more than her due share of such scoffings. As the vast walls of iron rose up on the bank of the Thames, amidst general admiration for the boldness and grandeur of the undertaking, a feeble croaking was distinctly heard saying—"Ah! they may finish it, though I dont believe they'll do that; but they never *can* get her into the water—why, dont you see? its as plain as a pike staff that if they try"—and so on. But the immense fabric steadily grew, and at last was ready for launching—and now came the delays and difficulty of the launch and the croak swelled into a triumphant shout of—"I told you so. I'm glad I've got no shares in such a hair-brained concern" until the ship satisfied her friends and for the time silenced her enemies by quietly floating off on a Sunday afternoon.*

---

* By the way it is rather remarkable that with one exception, all the epochs

The prophets of evil were almost annihilated when in spite of their dire predictions to the contrary, the great ship safely left the Thames, and they might perhaps have been silenced for ever, had not the unfortunate bursting of the funnel casing, in the saloon, set their tongues at work faster than ever. I must observe, that I think it says but little for the intellect of our people at large, that public confidence should have been so shaken, by an accident which might have happened anywhere, and the sole cause of which was instantly afterwards removed : but what will not prejudice do ?

The disappointment which the Portland (America) people experienced in 1859, caused them to write bitter things about the ship, but the New Yorkers had never done so, and now in June 1860, when they only thought of the excitement of welcoming so wonderful a visitor, their papers teemed with laudation and long accounts and descriptions of the ship. After several false alarms, I was informed about 2 o'clock on Thursday the 28th of June, that the "Great Eastern" was actually off Sandy Hook, and might be expected to arrive at the wharf prepared for her, at about 5 o'clock. I at once armed myself with a telescope, and proceeded to ascend the spire of Trinity Church, from which the bay is visible as far down as the "Narrow." I found a large party assembled on the tower, including several of the clergy; and on my appearance was hailed with, " Here's your big ship positively arrived after all." The population seemed to have taken to the roofs of their houses in all directions. Broadway was deserted save by a few figures rushing frantically to reach some spot commanding a view of the harbour. The Battery,

of the ship's history have occurred on a Sunday. She did not indeed sail from the Thames on Sunday, but she was launched on Sunday, sailed on her first Atlantic trip on Sunday, left the American Continent at Halifax, on her return, on Sunday, arrived at home on Sunday, and was safely landed on the Gridiron (where, at this present writing she rests,) on a Sunday. According to sailors' idea she ought to be a lucky ship.

and every spot from whence a view of the expected arrival could be obtained, was black with people. Afloat, too, the excitement was immense. Fleets of yachts and steamers crowded with passengers, were making their way down the harbour, to meet the monster. Near the Battery lay the frigate "Niagara," dwarfing, all the smaller craft, by her huge proportions. Presently some one cried, "I see her," and directly the six masts of the "Great Eastern" came into view above the point of land which juts out into the Narrows, on the Long Island side. Almost directly afterwards, her enormous hull appeared, entirely blotting out the small bit of horizon which is visible between the Long Island and Staten shores, the vessel at the same moment becoming shrouded in the smoke of the guns which were saluting her from the forts, and which she answered. She continued firing all the way up, in answer to the salutes, fired by the revenue cutter, "Harriet Lane" which kept company with her, and to the deafening cheers of the passengers on the deeply loaded Steamers which had gone to meet her, and which now followed her as fast as they could. In passing the "Niagara," she entirely eclipsed the huge frigate, dwarfing it to the apparent dimensions of a little barque of three hundred tons. Every ship dipped the ensign as she passed, and those which had guns, fired them; the Cunard Steamer "Asia" giving her a famous salute. The poor man in charge of the "Great Eastern's" ensign must have been tired, as he had to keep running it up and down, the whole way up past the wharfs. Amongst other friends of mine who witnessed the arrival from Trinity tower, was the organist of the Church, and after watching the Leviathan up to her wharf we descended, and at his suggestion, I sat down and played "God save the Queen" on the organ, with immense enthusiasm. As is usually the case here, the new attraction continued in high favour for a short time, and every one was loud in praise of the wonderful qualities of the great ship. The excitement has now, however, died out. The people are beginning to feel that they have been beaten; that the nose of the American eagle has been put decidedly out of joint, and, in short, they have become jealous. The other day on board, I overheard many disparaging remarks, such as, "Waal, I guess, she ain't no great chalks after all." "I reckon she don't come up to our 'Adriatic;' nohow you can fix' it," and "Talk of her great saloon! why my barn's better fitted up than that place." Then they found out that her deck was badly laid, (as indeed it unfortunately is), and they have certainly made the most of their discovery. The unlucky excursion to Cape May, of which you must have seen an account in the papers, has put the cope-stone to the downfall of the poor "Great Eastern." In justice to my American friends, I must admit that this kind of feeling is confined chiefly to the *mass*, among persons in good society I heard few remarks, which were not prompted by admiration of the wonderful vessel, and shame at the disgraceful manner, in which she, and all those connected with her, had been abused. She leaves New York on her homeward voyage, on the 16th of August; and if I am not incapacitated by sea sickness, I shall keep a Journal while on board; and I hope it may be more interesting than the scanty records of my last sea trip proved to be.

# JOURNAL KEPT ON BOARD "THE GREAT EASTERN."

*Thursday, the 16th August.* This was indeed a lovely day, and everything gave promise of a smooth, and speedy passage. At 2 o'clock, a small tug, which had been hired to convey the passengers on board, left the wharf and steamed out to the huge vessel, lying at anchor in the stream. We are but a small party, our number scarcely exceeding one hundred, and half of them are to leave us at Halifax. On arriving alongside we found that coaling was still going on, and the tug was therefore moored to one of the coal barges, over which we scrambled to the ladder, and were soon standing safely on the spacious deck of the great ship. The little crowd round the gangway, seemed lost on the huge space, which presented the appearance of a deserted street. I had secured a large and most comfortable state-room, opening off the First Dining Saloon; or, to speak more correctly, it is a suite of three state-rooms, opening off each other; a large one, eight feet by twenty, and two smaller ones, of which, I occupied one and my friend the other; while we had the beds in the large one folded up and concealed by curtains, thus making it a capital sitting room. Having seen our things comfortably arranged, I returned on deck and took up my station on the paddle box, in order to watch the evolutions about to be performed in starting the ship. We were lying with our head up the river, and a couple of powerful tugs were at hand, to render assistance, if required, in turning us round. About half-past four, the anchor having been got up with some difficulty, the screw engines made their first revolution, and we slowly began to move astern, till the bow of the vessel was pointed to the Jersey shore. At this time we were close alongside the "Adriatic," and (although the engines, both screw and paddle, were now turning ahead) in consequence of the stern way on the vessel, we remained nearly stationary for some minutes, during which time the "Adriatic" saluted with several guns ; her deck being crowded with spectators, as were also all the wharves, along the river. At last we were headed in the right direction, and the spires and buildings of New York began, with increasing celerity, to range astern. We were saluted by the "Persia" lying at her dock, and by the Cunard Screw Steamer "Australasian" which was on the point of starting for Liverpool. She was at anchor in the stream, and we passed close to her, our lofty bulwarks rising above the tops of her funnels. When off the Battery, which was crowded with people, we saluted with four guns, and then started off, full speed, down the bay. I now descended to dinner, in the first Dining Saloon, and having been told all sorts of dreadful stories as to the probability of my being starved, I was rather curious to see what kind of fare would be provided. Certainly there was not such variety as on the Cunard vessels, but everything was very good, and there was no cause of complaint, although several of our passengers, who could not make allowance for the many difficulties which must attend every department in the first starting of so gigantic an undertaking, grumbled a good deal. Although we were going at full speed, the motion of the engines was almost imperceptible, that of the paddle engines entirely so, and in the Grand Saloon, there was not the slightest vibration. On resuming my station on the paddle box, I found that we had passed the Narrows, and were nearing Sandy Hook. As we approached the Fort which lies opposite, our guns thundered out a national salute of twenty-one guns, and I confess I thought such an act of courtesy deserved a better return than the mere dipping of the Star and Stripes. They might have spared powder enough for one gun at least, but no! the poor Great Eastern had evidently lost her prestige, and although our gunners exerted themselves to such an extent as to let their rammer or spunge, or whatever it is, fall overboard—we received but a silent bow from the Fort. Our feelings were somewhat soothed by the vigorous cheering of a party in a little cockle shell of a boat, who all stood up, and, regardless of the strong chances of upsetting, gave us a grand ovation, to which our passengers responded by a general hoisting of pocket handkerchiefs. Having cautiously crept over the bar, we stopped and discharged Mr. Murphy, the New York pilot, the passengers giving him three cheers, and our brass band playing a medly of Yankee tunes : and at about 7 o'clock we started off, full speed, for Halifax. The sound of the bugle playing "Polly put the kettle on," reminded us that the kettle not only had been put on, but had boiled and made tea, and down we went to partake of it. It is difficult to imagine, in this lofty apartment lighted by five brilliant chandeliers, that we are at sea, everything is so unlike the general idea of a ship's cabin, and if this is the case in the Dining Saloon, much more is it so in the Grand Saloon, which, when lighted up, looks, with its superb mirrors, hangings and paintings, more like a tastefully furnished drawing-room, than the Saloon of a steamship. A word about this Grand Saloon. It was the fashion when it was first decorated to admire it, but I have lately heard, (especially in America) far more expressions of opinion adverse to, than in favour of it. Now it always struck me as being in its general decoration, one of the most beautiful, and truly artistic rooms I ever saw either afloat or ashore : it is not gaudy, it is gorgeous. The only fault which can be alleged against it is that perhaps the decorations are a little too delicate and fragile, to stand the rough usage to which they have been subjected. Evening Concerts have been proposed in the Ladies' Saloon, and after we have left Halifax, the Captain is going to organize one every evening, and there is plenty of material; for we have a good band, and there is not only an excellent piano in the Saloon, but also a professional pianist; hired specially for the delectation of the passengers. We are now exposed to the long swell of the Atlantic, but as yet our noble ship has not condescended to notice it, although she undoubtedly must roll if we encounter anything like a sea, owing to the extremely empty state of her inside. At night, the deck looks exactly like a long street, or rather two long streets running on either side of a block of houses, of which the smoking-room forms number one. By the time we retire for the night, the Great Eastern has fallen into her regular jog-trot swagger, it can hardly be called a roll ; it is just an easy, regular, motion by which, in order to avoid pitching and tossing on the one hand, or a rigid immobility on the other, she compromises matters with the waves of the Atlantic.

*August* 17*th.* I was rocked to sleep last night as if in a cradle, and rose this morning after a delightful slumber to find the lovely weather still continuing. It was very hot last night, and we find it a great advantage to be able to keep our windows open, in spite of any sea that may be running. No fear of water coming in at any of the ports on the upper and middle decks ; thirty feet above the surface ; indeed my window is nearly forty feet from the water. We have passed several vessels to-day, all of which altered their course, and bore down as close as they could to have a look at the monster ; one large American vessel paying us the compliment of lowering her topsails. Some of the passengers amused themselves by playing at quoits on the after deck, and succeeded by their uncertain aim in rendering that portion of the promenade somewhat dangerous: the chances being strong as the probability of some one finding an impromptu necklace in the shape of a quoit, round his neck. In the afternoon a little excitement was engendered by the giving way of one of the vangs of the fore-mast trysail gaff, which caused the heavy blocks to bang with a crash against the funnel at every roll of the vessel, and brought several ladies on the deck to see what was the matter. The derangement was most trifling, and the yard was secured in a few minutes; but an American passenger who was going to Halifax, was so frightened, that he said to me, "Well, I'm thankful I am not going across with you." Our speed, hitherto has been about fifteen knots, or nearly seventeen miles an hour; they mean to let out the floats of the paddles when we get to Halifax, so as to give them more immersion and a better hold on the water. In the evening, as we have as yet organized no concerts in the saloon, the gentlemen of our party congregate chiefly in the smoking room, and the ladies have their beautiful room pretty much to themselves.

*Monday, 20th* —— Saturday was as lovely a day as those which preceded it, and soon after breakfast we made out the land of Nova Scotia on the port bow, and just before descending to dinner which was at three, instead of 4 P. M., (the regular hour), we could discern Sambro Island right ahead. On returning to the deck after the meal was over, I found that we had rounded the island and were in the harbour, about six miles from Halifax. As we proceeded, I distinguished three steamers coming to meet us, crowded with people. The most advanced was the Cunard Company's screw steamship "Delta," having on board Mr. Cunard and a company of friends, and as we approached they rounded to, and gave us a hearty welcome, with cheers, and waving of handkerchiefs, the Delta firing two guns. I happened to be standing quite alone on the top of the port paddle box, and never shall forget the excitement which possessed me as I stood there waving my cap in answer to the cheers, which seemed specially meant for me ; and my vanity received a horrible blow, in the shape of a polite message from the Captain to the effect that he would be much obliged if no one would stand on the paddle-box. The Halifax people evidently had expected that the "Great Eastern" would creep cautiously up the harbour, and these steamers had intended accompanying us up to the town. They soon found out their mistake, for we left them all, though (the Delta especially) fast vessels, far astern, and steamed up full speed as far as George's Island, when we saluted with four guns. Each wharf as we passed (within a dozen feet) was crowded with people, who sent up deafening cheers, as the mighty vessel majestically glided past, while every available point of the houses and the citadel hill, was black with people. As soon as we were anchored, crowds of boats put off, and with numbers of sailing yachts surrounded us, the floating throng being soon joined by the Steamers which we had left behind, and the whole continued rowing, sailing, or steaming round the leviathan, their inmates cheering and shouting till their lungs must have ached. Amongst the crowd below, I soon espied some of my friends, who hastened up the side, and paying their half crown admission, put themselves under my guidance, and explored the vessel. We then went ashore, and I spent a delightful evening among my old friends, and returned on board at midnight. All night long the engineers' crew were at work inside the huge paddle boxes, altering the floats, and the work was not finished till 8 the following morning. We took on board here five passengers : among them, one of the great Wizards of the day, Professor Jacobs, and his brother, whose capital performances I dare say you may have seen ; as I think he has exhibited both in London and Edinburgh.

I was exceedingly disappointed at the shortness of our stay, having fully reckoned on spending a Sunday in my old quarters, and this feeling was in some degree common to me, and the whole of Halifax, many people having come 100 miles to see the ship, and then only getting a glimpse of her outside. At nine o'clock yesterday morning, (Sunday,) we were again in motion, and steaming out of the harbour, firing a salute of four guns as we started. A number of people were visible on the wharves, &c., watching our departure, and several little boats, filled with people, lay awaiting us further down the harbour, and as we passed, gave us their cheers and, I doubt not, good wishes. I stood at the stern, watching the rapidly receding town, which continued visible for nearly an hour, and then sending back my good wishes, turned away with a hope that I might again, at some future day, re-visit the place where I had passed so many happy hours. Our fine weather had forsaken us, and yesterday we had mist and rain, which rendered the lower regions more inviting than the deck. There was no service, and I spent a considerable portion of my day at the piano, in company with Handel. We are carrying across the Atlantic two very decidedly American fashions. We have a bar, and a barber's shop. All ocean steamers have a "bar" indeed, but the passengers generally take their tipple in the Saloon; here however those who want a stray glass of brandy and water must drink it at the bar. I believe the bar keeper has been taught how to make all manner of Yankee drinks, so that our American passengers (a very small number) can suit themselves to a nicety. The barber's shop is astern, off the third dining saloon, and has been very nicely fitted up; containing amongst other things a couple of regular American shaving chairs. The whole affair was got up by a smart little London hair dresser, who made a very good thing of it while the ship was in the States, though I do not think he has many customers amongst our present passengers. The wind and sea are now more ahead than previously, and though there is far more of both, our motion has rather diminished than increassd. A head sea is the Great Eastern's favourite kind of weather.

To-day we have the same style of weather, and in the course of the afternoon we were favoured with a fog, which rendered the deck untenable, and caused the dire necessity for blowing our steam whistle every now and then. We were somewhere in the vicinity of Cape Race, and stopped for soundings several times. In the course of the afternoon it began to be rumoured that Mr. Jacobs intended to give us a performance of magic, most probably the first time such an idea as a conjuring performance, on the broad Atlantic, ever entered the brain of man. Towards evening the rumour was confirmed, and all began to look forward with immense excitement to the novel entertainment. We had, for the first time, some music in the evening, though hardly a regular concert: some duets for piano and cornet à piston being very well played, by two of the "Great Eastern" professionals. Here am I, sitting on a luxurious velvet sofa, surrounded by splendid mirrors, rich silk hangings, and tasteful works of art: in a lofty and spacious apartment, brilliantly lighted by handsome chandeliers, while through the open doors of an adjoining and equally splendid room, is heard the domestic sound of the piano. All around me are seated groups engaged in reading, or a rubber at whist, or, if ladies, a little crochet perhaps. From such a description one would think I was an inmate of some grand mansion, the wealth of whose proprietor enabled him to administer most satisfactorily to the comforts of his guests, but —— I am in the cabin of a ship, and the ship is ploughing her way through the waves of the stormy Atlantic, on what would certainly be called, a "dirty" night. It seems ridiculous: it is like a story such as we might expect Baron Munchausen to favour us with.

When I recollect at intervals where I am, it makes my intellect stand amazed at the superb, the gigantic work of man's science and art which has brought to pass these strange anomalies. Many persons think, I dare say, that it is absurd to talk so, about a great mass of iron—a mere steamer. Such people have never crossed the ocean in the "Great Eastern," or if they have, they didn't deserve to, that's all I can say.

*Tuesday.*—This morning brought no sun with it, but on the contrary promised a duller and more disagreeable day than Monday : the wind too gives indications of shifting round, and bringing a beam sea with it, and many are the apprehensions that we shall have an increase of rolling, and a consequent stoppage of Mr. Jacobs' performance, which has now been announced, by numerous " posters," as intended to take place to-morrow. During the afternoon the decks, and especially the sides of the companion houses, became gorgeous with many coloured bills, of huge size, while smaller ones pervaded the passages below, all announcing the expected arrival of the wizard. Two special bills were made out for the occasion, and appeared pasted on one of the mirrors in the grand saloon, and also in the smoking room. In the evening we again had some music, though as yet no regular programme was carried out.

*Thursday,* 23*rd.*—Yesterday morning found our anticipations of increased motion realized, the ship was rolling decidedly more than previously, and there was every prospect of the weather becoming worse. But the wizard was not to be intimidated, and all day long there was a continuous procession of men carrying benches, flags, and lamps, along the decks, the whole being engulphed in the hatchway leading to the after-cargo space, where Mr. Jacobs intended to perform. Although our noble ship is most assuredly rolling, and at times pretty heavily, yet no one is sick ; there is none of that horrid *heave*, which is experienced in ordinary vessels, the deck merely tilts up, first one way and then the other, and causes no unpleasant sensation whatever, the only inconvenience being, the falling down of unsecured articles. We have, moreover, the consolation of knowing that any other ship would be pitching violently, and more than half her passengers sick, while the "Great Eastern" has never pitched a foot. At dinner and tea, the staple subject of conversation was, of course, the approaching entertainment, and at 8 o'clock I adjourned to the "Theatre." I found a "large and fashionable" audience assembled, all the passengers being present, and such of the officers as could be spared from duty, these occupying the front seats, while the back part was densely crowded by sailors, stewards, &c. The "Theatre" was a fine large hall, eighty feet by sixty, and fourteen feet high, and was elegantly decorated with flags, while from the roof hung a handsome chandelier, and a whole army of globe lamps, the engine rooms being despoiled of their lights, and left in darkness. In front of the stage was a row of foot lights, and a large mast head lamp, mounted on a chair. The stage was unfortunately fitted up at the side of the vessel, so that it was subjected to a far greater amount of motion, than if it had been placed against the tranverse bulkhead. The band occupied a corner at the left hand side of the stage, and after an overture, the curtain drew up and discovered the Wizard surrounded by all his paraphernalia just as I had seen him in New York. His trouble in unpacking and arranging all his things must have been immense, and we all felt that he was deserving of great praise, in taking so much trouble, for the amusement of his fellow-passengers, and the benefit of a public charity. I forget to mention that the entire proceeds of the entertainment were devoted to the "Dreadnaught" Hospital Ship. The performance proceeded with great success, the Wizard being assisted by his brother, who, in the character of an attendant Goblin, though in costume a "Buttons," contributed largely to the fun of the evening, by exciting laughter as well as wonder.

Meanwhile our motion still increased, and every now and then, during a heavier roll than usual, all breaths were held in the fear of some portion of the costly apparatus coming down: indeed my apprehensions of an accident, not only spoiled my enjoyment, but were fated to be realized, in the overthrow of a very ingenious and elaborate piece of mechanism, called the "Liliput Tavern," a sort of improvement on the inexhaustible bottle. But the Wizard took everything with the utmost good humour, and indeed, did not seem to be half as much discomposed, as his audience. How some of his tricks, difficult at all times, and almost impossible under existing, or rather rolling circumstances, were got through, I cannot imagine; but all went off without any further mishap. At the conclusion, Captain Hall got up, and proposed three cheers for Mr. Jacobs, which were given with a will, and the Wizard was bowing his acknowledgments, when the "Great Eastern" joined in the enthusiasm and gave a tremendous lurch, which sent us all bowing involuntarily, and produced an indiscriminate crash behind the scenes. As the crowd was at the moment engaged in making its way out of the Theatre, the confused heap into which all were thrown was decidedly amusing. I had the end of a bass fiddle stuck into my eye, but no one was hurt, and as the crash behind the curtain had been caused by the falling of some packing cases, and did not result in any breakage, we had a good laugh over the adventure. We were soon dispersed to our homes, the ladies for the most part retiring to bed: while the gentlemen proceeded to their favourite resort, the smoking room.

Mr. Jacobs' apparatus having suffered damage to the amount of some 10 or 12£., we proposed to him that the proceeds of the entertainment should in the first place be applied to repairing the damage, and if any surplus remained, that it should be given to the charity, but he would not consent to it, although urgently pressed to do so—so we made up a subscription to present him with a silver or gold snuff-box, on our arrival, and I suppose and hope that it will be done.*

*London, Monday.*—Thursday was the climax of our bad weather, we had a soaking rain, and a heavy rolling sea. From the lofty deck of this ernomous vessel it is impossible to estimate the size of the waves: it was only on descending to the lower deck, and looking from the ports, that I could tell through what a formidable sea we were cutting our way. The wind was favourable, and we had all our sails set, except the after main try sail, our speed being, for a considerable time, sixteen and a half knots an hour, (nearly nineteen miles,) the highest rate of speed which the vessel has ever made. What a shame it is that so disgraceful a deck should have been put upon this noble ship; it is to be renewed before she goes to sea again, and for very sufficient reason. During the morning we had a continual drip, drip, upon the carpet, and down the beautiful mirrors of the grand saloon, and a thick tarpaulin had to be spread all over the deck at that point to keep out the wet. The stewards seemed very careless too, and left the sky-lights half open, allowing a perfect deluge to pour down with the roll of the ship, though fortunately, it all went below into the lower deck, and did not injure the hangings, &c. of the upper saloon. During the afternoon, Captain Hall made up a programme for a concert in the evening, several of the passengers, myself among them, contributing to the general harmony. The Captain himself gave us some airs on the flute, very well played, and with great taste. During the morning of Friday, as I was engaged in finishing a sketch in my spacious cabin, the noise of the screw and the slight vibration caused by it suddenly ceased, and I, immediately afterward, heard the steam

---

* The subscription which amounted to some 30£ was expended in the purchase of a ring of gigantic dimension, bearing a variety of devices, among others, the great ship herself and an appropriate inscription.

blowing off. I of course supposed we had stopped altogether, as there was not the slightest sound or vibration, and my astonishment was great, on looking out of the window, to see the paddles in full play. Owing to some trifling derangement, our screw had to be stopped for a few hours, and so easily did the paddle engines work, that, as I before said, their motion was absolutely imperceptible in my cabin, only about forty feet removed from the paddle wheel. In the evening we had another concert in the saloon, Mr. Jacobs amusing the company, vastly, with a display of his wonderful power as a ventriloquist. On Saturday we observed smoke a-head, which was found to be that of the "Australasian," which left New York in company with us, and which had passed us during our stay at Halifax. We were now rapidly overtaking her, and by evening, she was far astern. This was to be our last night at sea, as we expected to reach Milford Haven the following afternoon. A lottery was formed amongst some of the passengers, the tickets being ten shillings each, and having marked on them the hours. The holder of the hour at which the pilot should come on board was to be the winner. A meeting was also held of the passengers, and an address drawn up for presentation to the Captain, expressive of our great satisfaction with the accommodation, and general qualities of the noble vessel, and also our sense of the courtesy and attention shown by the Captain and Officers. One or two grumblers, who had not found the cuisine according to their extremely delicate palates, had the stupidity, and bad taste not to sign the address. But their signatures were not missed. Early on Sunday morning, we sighted the Irish coast, and before breakfast was over had left it for astern, and were steaming across the Irish sea. The morning service was read in the grand saloon at eleven o'clock, and at three we dined. After dinner we all betook ourselves to the paddle-box, to watch for the arrival of the pilot: the bold rocky headlands at the entrance to Milford Haven, having been visible before dinner, and now close to us. At length a little boat was seen making for the ship, and all the holders of tickets, whose time had not already gone by, rushed to the entrance gangway, watch in hand. The poor man seemed quite bewildered and frightened as he looked up at the enormous fabric, towering above his little boat; the responsibility of having to guide her safely in, seemed to crush his faculties. His bewilderment was decidedly not lessened by the excitement caused by his arrival, and he gazed at the crowd of passengers with a glazed eye, little dreaming that the step of his foot on deck, decided the ownership of some 19 or 20 £. From him we learnt that the whole Channel Fleet lay at Milford, and that we should have to pass through them on our way to the anchorage. We proceeded at half speed, and soon a steamer was seen coming to meet us. She came under our stern, and then kept us company up to the anchorage, the people on board giving us hearty cheers. The harbour of Milford Haven stretches a considerable distance inland, and winds amongst lofty hills, on turning the base of one of which, we discovered the fleet at anchor. We had not expected any further recognition than the dipping of the ensign, and were astonished on drawing near the first ship, a frigate, to see her crew clustered all over every part of the rigging up to the very trucks. As we came alongside, a tremendous cheer burst from the crew of the frigate, her band at the same moment striking up Rule Britannia, and her ensign descending in courteous salutation. We were so taken aback that we stared in speechless wonder, and could not find breath to reply; but on looking ahead, and seeing the whole fleet evidently prepared to pay us the same complement, we shouted for our band, who tumbled up in haste, while the Captain and Mr. Bold (the financial manager) took up their stations on the summit of the paddle-box, to lead off our intended response. The same enthusiastic welcome was given us by the next ship, the "Algiers," 91, and this time we replied to the best of our ability, our band playing "God save the Queen." And so we passed through the fleet, each ship giving us a more enthusiastic welcome than another, the sailors in several instances, standing on the trucks and waving their hats. The fleet numbered eleven line-of-battle ships and two or three frigates, among the former, the "Royal Albert," 121, besides several of ninety-one guns; yet all were dwarfed to an insignificant size by comparison with the "Great Eastern;" whose tonnage indeed is nearly equal to that of the entire fleet. The hill above Pembroke was black with people, and considering the state to which our throats had been reduced, it was fortunate that their distance from us, precluded the possibility of exchanging any more shouting. We dropped our anchor, and saluted with four guns soon after six, and thus ended our voyage, which has been the most delightful I ever made. I felt sorry when the huge anchor plunged into the water. I could have enjoyed weeks more of the sea, under such circumstances, as those of our "Great Eastern" trip.

Most of the passengers preferred remaining on board till morning to enduring the discomforts of a railway journey by night, and we accordingly passed our last evening on the "Great Eastern," without any diminution of our numbers. The Great Western Railway Company had provided a special train to carry us through to London at reduced rate of fare, and accelerated rate of speed, starting at nine the following morning. There was some difficulty about the anchorage in the course of the evening, and a small tug was fastened to our stern, for the purpose of towing it round, a little way. It might as well have tried to tow round Ireland, the funnel of the thing got red hot, and we all expected it to blow up, but not an inch could it move the ship; the difficulty, I believe, was got over towards morning, by anchoring from the stern. I shall not here enter into any discussion as to the relative length of our voyage, or the speed of the ship; suffice it to say, that she is beyond all comparison superior to any vessel afloat in comfort, beauty, size, and safety, and quite equal to any in point of speed. Moreover, she can keep up her speed in all sorts of weather, a head sea makes no difference to her, and where an ordinary steamer would be pitching and tossing on her way at about seven or eight knots an hour, the "Great Eastern" cuts through the most formidable waves, at nearly her full speed.

After a hasty breakfast on Monday morning, we embarked in the tug, which had been pulling vainly at us during the night, and shoved off, having previously taken leave of the good Captain, and such of his officers as were known to each of us. I was fortunate enough to make the acquaintance of several, and can safely say that I never met on any vessel, so pleasant and gentlemanly a set. As we steamed rapidly away, we saw Captain Hall standing at the stern waving his cap in adieu, but he soon became invisible, and in quarter of an hour we landed at the Railway Station. Here we found our "special" waiting for us, the engine gaily bedecked with the British and American flags, and "Welcome to the Great Eastern." We did not get off till near ten, but so perfect were the arrangements, that we were not delayed once, beyond the places at which we stopped for water, and reached London, a distance of 300 miles in six hours, somewhat astonishing our American passengers.

# NOTES OF A SHORT TOUR THROUGH THE NORTHERN PRESIDENCIES.

Organ in Bombay Cathedral.

## CHAPTER I.

Madras to Beypore.  Voyage to Bombay.  Bombay.  Colaba Church. Cathedral.

THE scenery on the Madras Railway between Madras and Coimbatore is not particulary interesting, and is moreover so well known as to need no description, which is perhaps fortunate, seeing that the train in which the writer of these notes travelled to Beypore passed over that portion of the route by night, and he is consequently not in a position to record his impressions of much outside the railway carriage. It is an awful thing for a lone bachelor to find himself, as I did, shut up for the night with a family party, including an ayah and a baby in arms; but the next compartment (a coupé) being found to be empty, on reaching Arcot, the paterfamilias and I adjourned thither, and dined together to our mutual satisfaction. As neither of us was aware of the contrivance by which the back of the seat turns up and forms a sort of upper "berth," we passed the night without much comfort, sitting bolt upright in our respective corners. After passing Coimbatore, the train runs close under the spurs of the Neilgherries and the Koondahs, and many beautiful peeps of the hills may be had, though the rate at which the train descends the steep incline to Palghaut, renders it difficult to form much idea of the scenery. Before reaching Beypore, the Ponany river is passed on the left, and the Wynaad range becomes visible on the right:

but, although the railway skirts the coast for a considerable distance, the sea is not visible till within some four miles of Beypore, at which point a wide creek is crossed by a remarkably shaky-looking wooden bridge which creaks and groans under the train in an ominous manner. A new iron girder bridge is in course of construction at this place, and the works are under the care of the Superintending Engineer of the line in the district, Mr. Wilkinson, who has a very nice bungalow, prettily situated on a hill overlooking the creek, and commanding a fine view of the sea and the distant hills. It was my extreme good fortune to be the guest of this gentleman during the five days I had to wait for that fast sailing craft the British India Steam Navigation Co.'s steamship "Burmah." Beypore is some four miles beyond the bridge, and consists almost entirely of the houses, &c. in connection with the Railway. There is a hotel over the station and a reading room for the use of the Railway employés, which is, on Sunday, used as a church. For this, however, the Railway Company are not to be thanked, as no provision for the performance of any service is made by them; and the service which is performed every Sunday is read by Mr. Wilkinson, who also plays the harmonium, and has organized the whole thing entirely on his own responsibility. Should he by any chance leave Beypore, there would, in all probability, be no attempt to remind the people that they are professedly Christians, unless the Chaplain of Calicut should come over now and then. Under the present arrangement, he visits Beypore, I think, once in two months, and celebrates the Holy Communion.

The most unpleasant part of the whole journey to Bombay is the getting off to the steamer at Beypore. The boats are large clumsy affairs, and have no raised seats like the Madras masulah boats, nor the vestige of an awning. Our party were huddled together with the luggage and the servants and the water, and I might add the dirt, in the bottom of the boat, and a pull of good three miles under such circumstances, with a blazing sun overhead and nasty swell on, sufficient to knock the boat about a good deal, was anything but pleasant. The "Burmah," although shamefully slow, is a very comfortable vessel of about 1,000 tons. Her cabins are all under the poop, on each side of the saloon, and are very prettily fitted up; and there was nothing to complain of except the attendance at table, which was simply nil, and those who had not their own servants must have starved. The voyage to Bombay would be pleasant were it not rendered tedious by the number of stoppages at different places on the coast; few of which could be seen to any purpose, on account of our anchoring so far from the shore. One place was however an exception. At Carwar we anchored in a very pretty little harbour, shut in by hills, and with several islands at the entrance, on one of which is a light-house. It was intended that king cotton should have done great things for Carwar, and the place was supposed to be a sort of infant Bombay: these ideas however do not seem to have been confirmed.

Bombay harbour has been so often described that it needs no description here, and indeed I had been able to form a very fair idea of its appearance. There is an appearance of life and activity and money-making, which is very different to the somewhat sleepy aspect of Madras. The harbour was crowded with shipping, the usual number of vessels being augmented by the transports engaged for the Abyssinian Expedition; and on shore, the gas-lamps, and English omnibuses, the height of the houses, some seven or eight stories, and the comparative absence of vile smells are features for which we look in vain in Madras. The two most prominent buildings on entering the harbour, are S. John's Church on Colaba Point, and S. Thomas' Cathedral in the Fort, or rather what once was the Fort, as all the fortifications, &c. have been entirely removed, and it is now merely a quarter of the city, separated from the remainder by the Esplanade. Of the Bombay churches I visited four, namely the Cathedral, Colaba Church, Byculla Church, and Trinity Chapel. Colaba Church is, I fancy, the finest church in India, and as such merits notice before the others. It is situated near the end of a long tongue of land which forms the north western boundary of the entrance to the harbour, and was built as a memorial church to those officers of the Bombay army who fell in 1857; at least I think this was the case.\* The church consists of a nave eight bays in length, with aisles and a clerestory, and a chancel of three bays, without aisles; the tower and spire being at what should be the western end of the north aisle of the nave. The church however is built with the chancel at the west end. The exterior is spoilt by the glass in the windows being brought forward almost level with the wall, and there is not, except on the west or rather east front, enough decoration in the shape of mouldings, drip-stones, &c. My sketch will give a rough idea of the front, although, being drawn almost entirely from memory, it is in some respects incorrect, especially the carriage porch. The spire is a considerable height, close upon 200 feet, if not more, and is, together with the whole church outside and in, entirely of stone. The interior is really striking, and infinitely more ecclesiastical in appearance than any other church I have seen in India. In the first place it is very large; the nave must be at least 120 feet long, and the chancel upwards of 30, while the height to the ridge of the roof cannot be far short of 70 feet. The arches, especially the chancel arch, are supported on very solid clustered columns, the details of which are however very clumsy and faulty in design. The general style is early English, and the aisle windows are all lancets

---

\* This is a mistake. The church was erected as a memorial of the officers and privates who fell in the Affghan war.

arranged in triplets, the heads of all being filled with very
good stained glass, and the lower part with venetians. The
walls of the aisles are arcaded throughout their entire
length, something like the west front, and the clerestory
windows are lancets arranged in pairs and filled with cathedral glass. The west window (it is convenient to speak as
though the church stood east) is a triplet and is filled with
very good stained glass, as are also the east window of the
south aisle, and a window near the Font. The organ stands
at the east end of the north aisle, and hides the window on
that side. The chancel is lighted by three large single lancets on each side, filled with cathedral glass, and a large five
light geometrical window over the Altar. This window is
in a far later style than the rest of the church, but it does
not look at all offensive on that account, and is perhaps
better adapted for the display of the excellent stained glass
with which it is filled. The centre light represents at the
foot, the Crucifixion, and above, our Lord seated in majesty.
A large piece of the glass in the centre of this figure has
fallen out, and although a new piece to replace it has been
in the hands of some "Department" or other for a long
time, the chaplain has failed to induce the authorities to
have the window mended. The sill of this window, as well
as the side windows of the chancel, is at least 20 feet above
the floor, and the side walls beneath the windows are decorated with arcading within which are illuminated the names
of the officers in whose memory the church was built. The
shafts supporting this arcading are of polished marble, and
the wall surface, below, is decorated in polychrome. Unfortunately the space beneath the east window is an eye-sore.
It consists of three arches filled in with open brick-work,
such as may be seen in godowns, and beyond is a vestry,
built in that charming style with which we in India are so
familiar.

It is intended, I believe, that a reredos shall be erected when funds are forthcoming; at present the only decoration behind the altar is, or was, a large red cross, which originally formed part of the Christmas decorations.

The altar itself is very small and unworthy of so fine a church, but were it a little more raised, and backed by a handsome reredos, the east end would possess great dignity, as the whole of the constructional chancel is reserved as sanctuary, and contains only three sedilia of carved wood. The pulpit, a stone one of rather commonplace design, is fixed against the first pillar of the nave, and the prayer-desk is opposite; the choir seats being between these and the chancel arch, the organ, as before stated, occupying the corresponding bay of the aisle. The seats for the congregation occupy the next five bays, and at the second pillar from the entrance a very handsome rood-screen extends across the nave, leaving the two end bays empty, and as a sort of ante-chapel. This screen ought, in my opinion, to have been placed between the pulpit and prayer-desk, although it is seen to greater advantage where it is. It is of wrought iron, gilded and painted, and was entirely executed in the Bombay school of arts, to which institution it does great credit. I had nearly forgotten to mention that the floor of the sanctuary is laid with encaustic tiles of a rich pattern, harmonizing with the painting of the walls.

Most unfortunately the chaplain has been unable, as yet, to get up a surpliced choir, and the singing is in the hands of a volunteer choir, of which ladies are members. The organ is a very fair instrument by Holdich, I think. It has two rows of keys, a tenor C swell of seven stops, great organ of eight stops, and pedal bourdon, but was so frightfully out of order that it was impossible to make much of it. The church is excellent for sound, that is, for musical sound, as I fancy preachers have hard work to make themselves heard.

The great fault of the church is, that it is simply a reproduction of a large English parish church, without one single feature to adapt it to the climate of this country.

It is to be feared that my description of Colaba Church does it as little justice as my sketch of the West Front and the screen—but it must be remembered that both are from memory, and imperfections will, I hope, be pardoned. The Cathedral of Bombay is dedicated to S. Thomas, and is, externally, something like S. Mary's Church in the Fort at Madras, although considerably larger. The tower was, some thirty years ago, gothicised in the strictest meaning of the word, and a quasi gothic lantern added to it. Three or four years ago, a scheme was set on foot for entirely remodelling the whole church, which, as it then stood, consisted merely of a nave and aisles covered with a bomb-proof vaulting, a tower at the west end, but not the vestige of a chancel. It was proposed to erect a chancel with an organ chamber on the south side and a sacristy on the north, the east end being apsidal : and also to surround the entire building with verandahs, remodelling the windows and details. An entirely new west front was proposed, and a new tower and spire was to be erected, in the same style as the other alterations, namely, an adaptation of early English, with something of a French character about it.

Most unfortunately, however, the funds ran short, and after the erection of the chancel and organ chamber, together with the purchase of a new organ, the work came to a standstill, and so remains. The nave, which is in its original state, although built of brick plastered, is very massive, and might easily be made church-like by the application of a little judicious ornamentation : indeed an attempt has been made in this direction at the western entrance, where a handsome Norman arch has been built of stone—and the floor, under the tower, laid with encaustic tiles. There is also a very handsome pair of gates made of wrought iron, coloured and gilded. In the north corner stands a beautiful font of carved stone. The bowl is circular, and is enriched with medallions, containing different subjects, one of which, is I think, our Lord's Baptism. The font is supported on pillars with polished granite shafts and carved stone capitals, and would be an ornament to any church. It was made in London, and was presented to the Cathedral at the time the alterations were in progress. The interior of the nave and aisles is coated with chunam, but of a quality far inferior to that used in Madras, and as there is no clerestory, and the pillars supporting the roof are very large and heavy, the effect is decidedly gloomy. The new chancel opens into the nave by a gothic arch, which, together with all the new work, is of stone, and springs from columns of polished granite supported on corbels about 10 feet from the floor. The organ chamber opens into the south aisle by a similar arch, which is entirely filled with the decorated front of the organ. The windows of the apse are arranged in two tiers; and are decorated with small columns of polished granite, the vaulting of the roof being supported on larger shafts of the same material between the windows. The apse is, I think, nine-sided, and there are consequently 18 windows, which will be filled with stained glass when the funds are forthcoming—at present they are filled with white calico. The whole of the chancel, apse and organ chamber are roofed with a stone vaulting with richly moulded ribs, the plain surface of the vaulting being relieved by bands of grey stone.

Between the apse, which serves as sanctuary, and the chancel, there is an arch similar to that between the nave and chancel, and a third similar arch opens into the organ chamber. The sanctuary is raised three steps above the chancel, which is itself two steps above the nave: the altar is consequently well raised, although it does not stand on a foot pace. Round the apse, under the windows, there is an arcading intended to open into a verandah, but as this verandah is not yet built, the arcading has been filled in, and the only attempt at a reredos is the introduction of a little extra carving, and diaper work in the arches just behind the altar. Unfortunately, the funds available have been insufficient to provide proper furniture for the sanctuary and chancel, and the choir seats, &c., are all temporary. The altar is of wood, and very solid, it has only one rather shabby-looking red cloth cover; and behind it is a shelf on which stand two brass candlesticks. The candles in these are lit at evening service. The pulpit and prayer-desk are in the nave, opposite each other. They are both of carved stone, but the pulpit is far too high and large, and the desk faces *west*.

The Bishop's throne is in the south aisle, and consists of a chair and desk of dark colored wood, carved according to a design which seems to have been made by one of those people who think that nothing can truly be gothic in character, unless it bristles all over with spikes and little pinnacles.

The seats between the pulpit and desk, and the chancel face north and south, as in the Cathedral at Madras, and in the north aisle is placed the old organ. This instrument contains 2 rows of keys, viz., a great organ of 8 stops and a tenor C swell also of 8 stops, and has $2\frac{1}{2}$ octaves of Bourdon pedal pipes. It probably was a very fair instrument when in order, but it is now in a wretched condition. The new organ is the largest, and in some respects the finest, organ in India. The lower part of the case is of oak, and the upper part consists of open iron work beautifully wrought and gilded, supporting the large metal pipes. The front of the organ faces the chancel, but as the instrument stands back near the wall, the chancel front is not much seen, and the principal decorations have been expended on the side facing the aisle. This is exceedingly handsome, and is made up of the large metal pedal open diapason, the longest pipe being 16 feet in length and about 11 inches in diameter. All the interior work of the organ is excellent, the metal pipes, including the 16 feet diapason, being all of spotted metal and the wooden pipes of mahogany. The chief excellence of the instrument is the splendid pedal organ of 6 stops, and it is in this and in the possession of a C C swell that the organ excels any other in this country. The tone is sweet but not very powerful, the organ in the Madras Cathedral being certainly far more powerful and brilliant. For the sake of those learned in such matters, I give a list of the stops of the Bombay organ, which is, I think, correct. I had nearly forgotten to mention that the organ was built by Bishop, and cost £1,500, a large sum considering the number of stops.

*Great organ.*

| | |
|---|---|
| Open diapason ......... 8 feet. | Flute............ 4 feet. |
| Bell Gamba ............ 8 feet. | Twelfth ......... 3 feet. |
| Stopt bass, clarabella treble................ 8 feet tone. | Fifteenth........ 2 feet. Sesquialtera... 3 ranks. |
| Principal............... 4 feet. | Trumpet......... 8 feet. |

*Swell organ.*

| | |
|---|---|
| Bourdon............... 16 feet tone. | Fifteenth........ 2 feet. |
| Open diapason...... 8 feet. | Oboe............ 8 feet. |
| Stopt diapason...... 8 feet tone. | Cornopean....... 8 feet. |
| Principal............. 4 feet. | |

*Choir organ.*

| | |
|---|---|
| Stopt bass, clarionet Flute.................. 8 feet tone. | Flute............ 4 feet tone. Principal......... 4 feet. |
| Keraulophon (Tenor C)...................... 8 feet. | Piccolo........... 2 feet. Clarionet (TenorC) 8 feet |
| Dulciana................ 8 feet. | tone. |

*Pedal organ.*

| | |
|---|---|
| Stopt Bass (wood)...16 feet tone. | Principal metal... 8 feet. |
| Open Bass (wood)...16 feet. | Fifteenth metal... 4 feet. |
| Open Bass (metal)...16 feet. | Bombardon metal.16 feet. |

There are 7 couplers and 9 composition pedals. I was unable to attend a morning service in the Cathedral, but was present at evensong several times. There is a large surpliced choir numbering some 18 or 20 boys, and about 10 or a dozen men, chiefly volunteers. At present there is no paid organist, and it is doubtful whether the funds at the disposal of the Cathedral authorities will enable them to engage one for some time. Meanwhile they have been most fortunate in finding several gentlemen willing to act as organist, and as a choir master is provided, things have gone on very creditably. The chanting of the psalms was decidedly good, and the whole service done "decently and in order." There was, at one time, a weekly celebration in the Cathedral, but to the great disgrace of the authorities, this has been given up. It is difficult to understand what excuse can be given for such a course, unless indeed the congregation refused to attend, in which case the disgrace rests on their shoulders. I had forgotten to mention that there is a library belonging to the Cathedral. This occupies a room over the vestry, at the west end of the south aisle.

Bombay Cathedral is so closely surrounded by very tall houses that, even if the proposed alterations were carried into effect, it would not be an imposing building. Its present external appearance is most deplorable. The small enclosure in which it stands is full of dirt and rubbish, in the midst of which, opposite the west door, is a handsome fountain, looking strangely out of place. The external wooden roof of the apse is not finished, and the vaulting is covered with mats and tarpaulin, as a defence from the destructive effects of the weather. Just behind the Cathedral are the enormously tall new buildings which compose the "Elphinstone Circle"—and the contrast between their spruce and bright appearance, and the dreary and ruinous aspect of the Cathedral, suggests that in Bombay the worship of Mammon is more cared for than that of God.

The design of the Elphinstone circle is very far from faultless, and I believe the construction of the houses is far from solid, but they are faced entirely with stone, and, together with the Town Hall, make up a piece of street scenery by no means despicable. The High Court is also in the Fort, but is a most wretched-looking building—and the same remarks may apply to the Kirk in connection with the Scottish Establishment.

Byculla Church is somewhat in the style of Christ Church, in the Mount Road at Madras, though far more decently arranged. There is no chancel, but the altar stands in a recess at the east end. It is of very fair size, and I think there is a credence table.

The organ (a small instrument) is in the west gallery. The service is of the "good old Protestant" type, and the singing, considering that nearly all the boys of the Byculla School always attend the church, cannot be commended. The chaplain has, ready to his hand, all the materials for getting up an excellent choir, but it does not seem to be considered worth while. Trinity Chapel is situated in the very heart of the most populous part of the city, and is, externally and internally, by no means ecclesiastical in its appearance. In it, however, Catholic truth is boldly taught, and in connection with it, a great deal of hard missionary work is gone through by its excellent priest—the Rev. C. Gilder. It is, I believe, the only church in Bombay where there is a weekly celebration of the Holy Communion—and although, owing to an utter absence of funds, a regular choir has not been organized, the very utmost that is possible is done to make the services orderly and decent.

I attended an early celebration, and observed that the celebrant (Mr. Gilder) who was assisted by the Rev. C. Kirk' occupied his right place at the north side, not the north end of the altar, while the Deacon stood below the foot pace, facing east. I believe that they have occasionally, on festivals, had choral celebrations, so far as the limited means at their disposal admitted of. The building itself is merely a large upper room with square windows, wooden pillars, and a gallery at one end, in which at one time stood an organ. This, however, long since became useless, and has been removed; a harmonium is now used, and is placed near the altar. The only other place of worship, in connection with our church, that I could hear of in Bombay, is a small chapel built by the P. and O. Company, near their dockyard at Mazagon, for the use of their employès.

# CHAPTER II.

Bombay continued. Towers of Silence. Malabar Hill. Elephanta. Regatta in the harbour. Bhore Ghaut.

THE Government House of Bombay is situated at Parell, which is quite seven miles from the Fort, and in the neighbourhood there are many very nice houses. Government House stands in a large compound at the foot of Parell Hill, from the top of which there is a magnificent view of the harbour. Parell is, however, too far from the business part of Bombay to be the favourite place of residence, and most of those who can afford to pay the enormous rents charged, have houses on Malabar Hill, which is a narrow ridge forming the northern boundary of the now famous "Back Bay;" Colaba Point forming the southern boundary and separating the Back Bay from the harbour. At the extreme point of Malabar Hill is a house occupied occasionally by the Governor, and very near this on the northern slope of the hill there is a most curious and interesting temple, or rather a small city of temples. The houses and temples are clustered round a large tank, and the lanes intersecting the crowded mass of buildings are exceedingly picturesque. The whole of this little colony is enclosed by walls, and as it stands on the steep slope of the Hill, the streets and lanes consist chiefly of long flights of stairs. What makes this quaint little place seem still more striking is, that the roads and houses on Malabar Hill have an eminently nineteenth century sort of appearance, and

West front of Colaba Church.

the sudden plunge out of European civilization into such a very oriental and primitive-looking place as this little city of temples is rather startling. At the other end of the Hill there is another group of buildings of a very different and rather more objectionable nature than these. I refer to the Parsee "Towers of Silence," the presence of which, in the very midst of the principal European residents, cannot be considered other than an intolerable nuisance. The external appearance of one of these is very much that of a large gasometer painted white. The building is generally about fifty feet high, and perhaps fifty or sixty in diameter, and always circular. On a huge platform some 3 or 4 feet below the parapet, the Parsee dead are exposed to be devoured by the vultures which sit perched in flocks on the cocoanut and palmyra trees which surround the towers. I fancy that no actual annoyance is caused to the residents, as it is believed that a body seldom remains for more than half an hour. Still the idea is horrible, and the sight of the gorged, disgusting looking vultures is enough to make one sick.

The view from the Hill is very fine, extending across Back Bay, and including Colaba Point, Bombay, the harbour, with its shipping—the islands of Elephanta and Salsette, and the distant hills toward Matheran: the situation is very cool and pleasant moreover—but the rents charged for the houses are simply scandalous. For a house which would cost about 80 rupees a month in Madras, no less than 500 rupees are paid on Malabar Hill; and there is one house which lets for rupees 1,800 a month.

Few people leave Bombay without paying a visit to the caves of Elephanta, and a very enjoyable trip may be made thither. The island of Elephanta is situated in the harbour, a little above Bombay, and about six miles from the P. and O. Company's dock at Mazagon. It consists of two hills about 500 feet in height, with a narrow gully between them, and in this the caves are situated. The whole island is thickly wooded, and the pathway up to the entrance of the principal cave is paved with stone, and there are, at intervals, long flights of steps. We had a long and somewhat wearisome pull against wind and tide, and when we reached the island, the water was too low to allow the boat to approach within 100 yards of the shore, and we had to be carried ashore in a somewhat undignified fashion. The task of climbing up the steep pathway, or rather staircase, above mentioned, was no joke, in the hot sun, and very thankful we were to reach the cave, which we found deliciously cool. The principal cave is nearly square, and measures, I should think, some 70 or 80 feet each way. The roof, which is of course the solid rock, is supported by five rows of columns, some of which have fallen, and the height is about 17 or 18 feet. On each side of this cave are other excavations, partly open to the sky, and everywhere there are rude and uncouth carvings of different Hindu deities, which I am not sufficiently "up" in Hindu mythology to describe. I fancy most of the visitors to Elephanta come there, on picnics intent, although an occasional daub of red paint on the figures, especially on one with an elephant's head, seems to indicate that the cave is still resorted to for the purpose of worship. There is a European pensioner in charge of the place, and chairs and tables are provided for those who wish to take tiffin or breakfast. We enjoyed the latter meal immensely, sitting near the entrance, with a glorious view of the harbour and the Island of Salsette before us. We, in Madras, would give something to have so charming a spot within easy reach of us, although the beauty of Elephanta is deceitful to some extent, as the island is so unhealthy, that no one can live there for any length of time. We enjoyed a pleasant sail back to Mazagon, and therein tasted another of the delights of Bombay, for which we sigh in vain in Madras. The harbour of Bombay is certainly most lovely, and the inhabitants make the most of it, and get as much pleasure out of it as they can. There was a grand regatta during my stay, in which all manner of craft, from fine schooner yachts of 200 tons down to canoes, took part. The stewards were fortunate enough to secure the " Queen" (a splendid steamer of 3,500 tons) as the flagship, and some 400 invitations were issued to a tiffin or dinner on board, and a dance afterwards. I fancy however that admissions were not strictly limited to the holders of these tickets. I was never asked for the one I received, and I am sure there must have been nearer than 600 than 400 people on board. The result was a desperate scramble after both eatables and drinkables. We did not remain for the dancing, and we heard afterwards that, a considerable quantity of champagne having been surreptitiously imbibed by the ship's crew, the proceedings were terminated by something rather approaching the nature of a "shindy."

Being very anxious to see the works on the celebrated Bhore Ghaut, we took tickets by the morning train for Kandala which is at the head of the incline. The scenery on the line between Bombay and the foot of the ghaut, a distance of 70 miles, is extremely pretty, the hills both near and distant appearing every minute under fresh and more beautiful aspects. At one station (Callian I think) I noticed a very pretty little gothic brick building—it is, I believe, a dispensary, and was built from the design of Mr. Paris of Bombay. At present, the lower part of the Bhore Ghaut* incline is impassable for passengers, on account of the fall of a viaduct, and the train therefore runs, on a level, nine miles beyond the beginning of the incline to a station imme-

---

* This has since been repaired.

diately below the reversing station, up to which the passengers have to make their way on foot or in palanquins. The break vans and luggage vans however are taken up the incline as far as the broken viaduct, where they are conveyed by temporary rails across to the opposite side. Here another engine awaits them, and they meet the passengers at the reversing station. We were enabled, through one of the Railway officials, to travel in the break van by this route, and thus obtained a view of the whole incline. It is about as exciting a bit of railway travelling as can well be imagined ; tunnels and viaducts succeed each other in quick succession, and every now and then the train skirts the very edge of a precipice 1,000 feet high. The total rise from the foot of the incline to Kandala is some 1,800 feet, and this ascent is accomplished, when the road is entirely open, in about an hour, the distance being about 14 miles. The engines employed on the incline are of immense power. They have no tenders, the water-tank being over the boiler, and they run on 8-coupled wheels. Notwithstanding their power, they occasionally stick fast with a heavy train, which was the case with us. We came to a stand-still about a mile below Kandala, where the incline is about the steepest, namely, 1 in 35. The horrid thought at once suggested itself : " If we were to run back ?" what then ? We certainly could not get out, for the doors were carefully locked. There is however no real danger, as the powerful breaks used are quite sufficient to keep the train stationary. The view down the Ghaut from Kandala is very beautiful, the numerous viaducts of the Railway adding to its beauty. It seems almost incredible that a train should be able to climb such an ascent, but one soon ceases to wonder at anything now-a-days. I saw two buildings near the station at Kandala which looked like churches, but we had no time to visit them, as we returned to Bombay the same afternoon.

# CHAPTER III.

Bombay to Nagpore. Church at Nagpore. Nagpore to Jubbulpore. Marble rocks. Jubbulpore to Allahabad. Church at Allahabad.

THE railway journey from Bombay to Nagpore, a distance of 520 miles, is very fatiguing, occupying, as it does, thirty hours. We left Bombay at 6 P. M., and therefore passed the most interesting part of the line, the Thull Ghaut, at night; although as it was bright moonlight we were able to make out the general features of the scenery. This incline is very similar to the Bhore Ghaut, the same succession of tunnels, viaducts and fearful-looking abysses—and there is also a reversing station, where two or three years ago a frightful accident happened. A train, having at the top of the incline overshot the commencement of the steep gradient, soon acquired a speed which could not be controlled, especially as the engine was not under steam at the time—and on reaching the reversing station, the whole train leapt over the precipice, and was dashed to atoms. There is one circumstance which lends a pleasing little excitement to the travelling on the G. I. P. Railway, and that is, the knowledge that nearly all the viaducts are unsafe or doubtful. Throughout the latter part of the journey near Nagpore, almost every bridge was under repair, and the train had to pass along temporary rails, down one side of whatever had to be crossed and up the other. Nagpore is decidedly a prepossessing looking place. The roads are excellent and the compounds large, and well kept—there are also large, spreading trees in abundance. The Church has only recently been consecrated—and is in some respects a pretty one. It is unfortunately only of brick plastered, but the design is by no means bad. It consists of a nave with verandahs, transepts, chancel and tower, (on the south side of the chancel). There is, at the west end, a large carriage porch. The verandahs of the nave are, in effect, aisles with solid looking buttresses, and boldly-moulded arches. They open into the nave by doors. The roofs are of good pitch and are ornamented with an iron cresting—the roof of the porch being nearly as high as that of the nave. The east wall is double and in the inner wall is the east window with an exact *fac simile* of it, mullions, tracery and all, in the outer. The space between the two is about six feet, and this arrangement is of course designed to shade the window. The tower is not carried higher than the spring of the chancel roof, but is designed to have a tall spire. Internally, the church appears to have been intended to be fitted with choir seats between the transepts, one of which would afford a capital place for an organ. There did not appear to be any provision for a choir however, and the harmonium was placed at the right hand side of the west door.

The altar is pretty well raised, and the window above it is filled with stained glass representing the Crucifixion. The pulpit is, I think, a stone one, but I am not sure; indeed our visit to the church was so hurried, that I have by no means done it justice. It has the merit of being lofty, and the roofs are of open woodwork, stained a dark colour.

The distance from Nagpore to Jubbulpore, where the Railway again becomes available, is about 160 miles. The road is good and the scenery in some places very pretty, although no where grand. No one can complain of any want of excitement during the journey, seeing that the general behaviour of the horses which are supplied to luckless travellers by that route, is such as to keep the occupants of the coach in constant anxiety for the safety of their necks. We were fortunate enough to accomplish our journey in 36 hours, without an upset; but two travellers who had left the day before, got a disastrous tumble, their coach rolling over several times and alighting on its roof with the wheels in the air! A solitary individual, who left Nagpore an hour or so before us, appropriating, I have reason to believe, the conveyance which had been prepared for us, met with a just retribution, for we passed him about a couple of miles beyond Kamptee, sitting helpless in his coach at the foot of the embankment, his horses having dragged him off the road and down into the fields, whence he had to be dragged up by bullocks. Our coach was comfortable enough, being a wide, roomy palanquin coach with plenty of space for two people to lie at full length. We carried a considerable amount of luggage on the roof, which rendered the whole concern top heavy, and we were on the very verge of an upset more than once. No words can convey any idea of the unmitigated disgust inspired in us by the dreadful character of the horses. We changed them every five miles, but only three or four times did we get any that did not either attempt to run off the road, or refuse to proceed at all. I have since heard that we were on the whole fortunate, as sometimes a fire had to be lighted under the horses before they would stir, and that they revenged themselves by just moving far enough to bring the coach comfortably over the fire, and then stopping. We had no time to stop at Kamptee, which is about seven miles from Nagpore. The roads and compounds reminded me of the Luz, or the Adyar at Madras, shady, and well kept. The public gardens also looked very pretty. They are close to the Church, which is, externally, in the usual D. P. W. style. Internally, however, I believe it is very nicely fitted up with a well raised Altar, choir stalls, and other requisite Church furniture. On this road two rivers have to be passed, the second (the Nerbudda,) which is crossed about four miles before reaching Jubbulpore, being as yet unbridged. The passage of this river was about the most disagreeable part of the journey : the river was low, and the coach had to be dragged by four bullocks half way across its bed, through deep sand and occasional patches of shallow water, before reaching the deep channel. Here we were, with infinite difficulty, embarked on board a ferry boat, and on disembarking, bullocks again came into requisition to drag us up the steep bank of the river. Our last stage into Jubbulpore was performed with the most abominable pair of horses we had yet seen, they ran away with us down a very steep piece of road, ending in an extremely awkward bridge, on the very edge of which they were most fortunately pulled up. After this display of activity, these charming quadrupeds could only be induced to proceed at a very slow walk the rest of the journey. It took us upwards of an hour to perform the four miles from the Nerbudda to Jubbulpore, which place we reached at about midnight, finding to our intense disgust that our choice of beds lay between the top of the billiard-table, and the floor under it.

We had unfortunately too little time at our disposal to see much of Jubbulpore, which is, I believe, a favourite station, and judging from what little we did see, deservedly so. The entire day following our arrival was devoted to a visit to the " Marble Rocks." The place that goes by this name is a narrow ravine, through which the Nerbudda flows between perpendicular rocks, some eighty or ninety feet in height, and composed entirely of marble, which, although weather-stained and black in many places, is very beautiful, especially when the projecting crags and pinnacles, which resemble those of an iceberg, are lit up by the brilliant sunlight. The "Marble Rocks" are about twelve miles from Jubbulpore, but would be worth going to see, were the distance twice as great. It was late in the afternoon before we left them, and the scene was quite unlike anything I had before witnessed, as we were rowed along the deep and narrow channel which the river has cut for itself between these perpendicular marble walls. The channel is about half a mile long, and winds considerably, so that we and our boat seemed completely shut in from the outer world. The rays of the declining sun could not penetrate to the surface of the water, which, together with the lower parts of the rock, was shrouded in semi-obscurity—the white marble peaks above shining out with dazzling brilliancy by contrast. I find myself getting quite poetical : the sentiments of that nature, which inspired us in what the guide-books call "The Marble Home of the Nerbudda" did not, however, prevent us from indulging in some brandy and water, the latter fluid being supplied by the Nerbudda itself, and deliciously cool, as if ready iced.

We left Jubbulpore the day following, by railway for Allahabad. The distance is about 250 miles, and is performed in about 14 hours. The road, which is newly opened, is very good ; but many of the stations are unfinished, and the delays which occurred at most of them were very vexatious. Allahabad is situated at the junction of the rivers Ganges and Jumna, and the Railway is carried across the latter river by means of a magnificent iron girder bridge, nearly a mile in length. There are, on the East Indian Railway, three of these great bridges, much resembling each other. The other two are that which crosses the Jumna at Delhi, and the celebrated Saone Viaduct, on the line between Benares and Calcutta. We reached Allahabad late on a Saturday evening, and as we had arranged to leave the following day by the afternoon train for Delhi, we had little time to do anything but go to church. We found the church a plain building, like the church at Byculla, but with a very deep chancel. There is also a wooden rood-screen in a quasi-Gothic style, having a small cross in the centre. The chancel is fitted with choir seats, and clergy stalls, the pulpit being placed outside the screen in the nave. The altar is of good size and well raised, and behind it was a temporary reredos of evergreens, which appeared to be a remnant of the Christmas decorations; though why remaining up in Lent I know not. The east window is filled with stained glass, the subject of which I forget, and on the south side of the sanctuary, which is railed off and handsomely carpeted, are sedilia for the celebrant and his two assistants. The sight of a Credence-table, also reminded us that we were now in the favoured Diocese of Calcutta, where this article of Church furniture must always, by order of the Bishop, be provided. There were a few boys in the lower seats of the chancel, but they were not surpliced; and the principal part in the singing was taken by a choir of ladies and gentlemen, who occupied the back seats. The service (Morning Prayer, followed by celebration) was not choral—the Canticles only being chanted, and the *Te Deum* was used, although the season was Lent. The celebrant, I *think* consecrated in front of the Altar, and there was an immense number of communicants. I need scarcely say that the boys marched out after the Prayer for the Church Militant, but although all the other members of the choir remained, neither the Sanctus nor Gloria in Excelsis were sung. There is no organ, the singing being accompanied by a harmonium. One would think that in a large station like Allahabad, funds might easily be obtained for getting a fair-sized organ. There are, I believe, two other churches in the place ; but we could not find time to visit them—indeed, I was unable even to go to the Fort, which is, I understand, worth seeing. It is close to the bank of the Jumna, which is here a magnificent river, a third of a mile or more in width. Allahabad is an important station, and will become more so in future, now that the Government Offices, hitherto at Agra, are to be removed thither; but it is not by any means a cheerful-looking place, and shady trees, which are so abundant at Nagpore and Kamptee, are here altogether wanting. Our next halting-place was Delhi, of which I shall be able to give a more detailed account than this very meagre one of Allahabad.

# CHAPTER IV.

*Delhi—Railway Station—Fort—Palace—Station Church—S. Stephen's Memorial Church.*

THE railway journey from Allahabad to Delhi is about as tedious and uninteresting a piece of travelling as need be. The scenery is simply an unvarying and unbroken flat country, by no means well wooded—the speed of the train is not more than 25 miles an hour, the distance of upwards of 500 miles being performed in a little over 20 hours, and the dirt, what with coal dust and ordinary dust, exceeds anything I ever met with on any railway.

Just before reaching Delhi, the train crosses the Jumna by a magnificent bridge, very similar to that at Allahabad, and immediately enters within the walls of the city,—the contrast between the railway works and the huge masses of dark red stone fortification and gateways, with their very Eastern looking cupolas and kiosks, being very striking. The railway enters the city close to the Fort, and from the windows of the carriage can be seen, on the left, the white marble buildings of the Palace perched on the edge of the walls. The railway station, which is as yet unfinished, is being built in the same style as the old buildings which surround it, and will be handsome and substantial, though perhaps unconsciously the architect has imparted a very decided dash of the English mediæval style to what is probably intended to be oriental: on the other hand, this may have been done on purpose, and if so, with some reason. Close

Memorial Church Altar—Delhi.

to the station there is a small church, built, I believe by the Railway Company. It is in a sort of Italian round arched Gothic style—with nave, chancel, and transepts, the chancel and transept both being apsidal. The building is, however, too small and toy-like to be effective.

To see all that should be seen in and about Delhi would take far more time than we were able to afford, and consequently, I have but a hazy idea of the many buildings and places of interest which abound in the city and its environs. The Fort is generally the first resort of visitors, as it contains the celebrated Palace, with which I fancy most people are sadly disappointed. The whole city is entirely surrounded by fortifications, and the Fort is situated at that part which faces the Jumna. Most of the gates of the city, including the now famous Cashmere gate (which was close to our hotel), are small insignificant structures of brick, in some cases faced with red stone; but the gateways of the Fort are magnificent buildings of red stone, or at least faced with it, and ornamented with marble. They are all much alike, having two lofty octagonal towers, surmounted by white marble cupolas, the gateway being between the towers. The whole structure is so lofty, that although the gateway itself is some 40 feet high, there are two or three stories above, all more or less ornamental. The principal gateway leads into a long vaulted arcade, something like, and nearly as large as, the nave of some Gothic cathedrals. The details however are not exactly those of a Gothic cathedral, being meaningless and coarse to a degree; and indeed, after the magnificent gateway, this vaulted hall, or whatever it may be called, is disappointing—and on emerging from it, we found ourselves in a large open space or esplanade, which appeared to be in a state of chaos. Buildings old, new and unfinished, seemed as though dropped down promiscuously all over the place, but nothing appeared in a finished or orderly state. I confess to great disappointment with the Palace. No vestige of a garden remains; and the buildings are now surrounded by barracks, and intersected by roads. The principal portion of the Palace consists of three white marble pavilions, which stand in a line on an elevated platform overlooking the river. They are in very good preservation, and display internally much decoration in the shape of richly carved marble screens, and beautifully inlaid work: close to these is a beautiful little mosque, with a small court-yard, entirely built of white marble, with the exception of the external walls, which are covered with slabs of red stone. The mosque itself is in the usual form, with three domes and two slender minarets—these being all of the purest white marble with richly gilded finials; but the whole structure is a mere toy, not measuring more than 40 or 50 feet square, including the court. The great hall, in which stands the famous "peacock throne," is a very common-place looking building of brick plastered, and is used as a barrack. At one time it was no doubt surrounded, together with the marble buildings, by gardens; but of these no traces remain, the very last tree visible, being cut down on the day of our visit, in order that a report as to the existence of some treasure buried under it, might be verified. I believe that nothing whatever was found. The "peacock throne" stands on one side of the hall, and is made of white marble. It was formerly inlaid with gems, but these have all been picked out, and now that the deed has been done, the throne is enclosed in a species of iron cage, to prevent, it is to be supposed, some one from walking off with it bodily. As, for very shame's sake, I should be sorry to see any description, however feeble, of the "Jumma Musjid" or great Mosque of Delhi, figuring on the same page with what I have to say regarding the buildings which the "Sahib Logue" consider good enough for the worship of Almighty God, I will defer my remarks concerning the mosques, &c, and endeavour to give some idea of the churches of Delhi.

I visited two of these, the Station Church, near the Cashmere gate, and the new Memorial Church, S. Stephen's. The first named of these has been designed, apparently, after Sir Christopher Wren's model of his original design for S. Paul's Cathedral in London, but it is not *quite* so large as S. Paul's and is built of brick and plaster, instead of stone. The redeeming feature of the exterior is a large gilt cross which surmounts the dome, although even this is open to objection, as provoking a contrast between the costly and beautiful marble domes which support the crescent, and the paltry stucco dome which is considered quite good enough to uphold the cross. Internally the church is peculiar, to say the least of it. It is circular, but has a small square chancel, with *two* east windows, between which stands the altar. The ecclesiastical authorities have some sense of decency however, and nothing offensive is to be found in the arrangements. There are choir stalls and a harmonium, and of course a credence table. The two east windows, which are common circular-headed windows without mullions or tracery, are filled with very curious-looking stained glass. One represents, I think, the Crucifixion, but the general effect of the glass is not good, and at first I thought the pictures were painted on coloured window blinds. I could not discover whether there was a weekly celebration at this church, though I fear not ; and I do not think there is a surpliced choir.

The Memorial Church is in every respect far more satisfactory than the other. It is built of brick, with red stone dressings, in the round-arched Italian Gothic style, and has many good features. Externally, it appears as a simple nave with an apsidal termination, verandahs, and small campanile at the west end. The west door is handsome, and so are the verandahs, both being of red stone and rather profusely decorated with carving; but the campanile is far too small and plain, and looks more like a factory chimney than anything else. Internally, there is much to commend, and much to condemn, though fortunately the commendation refers to matters the most important.

There are no aisles, but the verandahs open by large doors into the church, and serve the same purpose. The eastern bay of each is enclosed, and serves on the north side as a vestry, and on the south as an organ chamber, in which is placed the harmonium. There is no chancel screen, nor is the separation between nave and chancel marked, otherwise than by the substitution of small lancet windows (in two tiers), for the doors above mentioned. The altar is of good size, and is backed by a reredos of white marble, simple, but, on the whole, effective in design. There is a credence-table, and the altar was, on the occasion of our visit, vested in a handsome frontal and super-frontal of dark blue velvet, with orphreys of silver lace. I at first thought that this must be the Lent violet cloth; but I found that it was the only one the church possessed.

There is here a surpliced choir, who sing Gregorians with Hindustani words! I did not hear them, but I heard the organist play on the harmonium,—and if the singing is as good as his playing (he was a native lad of 17 or 18), it must be very creditable. At the west end there are two fonts—one made in the shape of a coffin, and of the same size, to typify, I suppose, the "Death unto Sin." It did not appear what distinction was made, or who was baptized in the coffin-shaped font, and who in the other. In an evil moment, the people connected with this church seem to have delivered the interior walls over to the tender mercies of some one who thought he had a talent for mural painting. The result is, that the walls are painted a very ugly light slate colour, and round the apse there are coarsely painted shields, bearing the emblems of the Apostles and Evangelists. The idea is good, no doubt; but the execution is detestable. The windows, with the exception of the west window which is circular, are all lancets, and are filled with grissaile glass. On the whole, this little church is something to be thankful for, though I confess that the contrast between our churches and the glorious buildings of the Mahometans in Delhi, and more especially in Agra, made me very savage indeed. I believe there is a weekly celebration in S. Stephen's, and the services are, so far as is possible, choral. I observed moreover that there were no kneeling cushions at the ends of the altar; but in front of it was a mat, and on the step below two others, so that it may reasonably be presumed that the Priest celebrates "in medio Altaris."

## CHAPTER V.

#### Jumma Musjid—Kootub—Cashmere Gate—Arrival at Agra.

As these notes were intended to be almost exclusively devoted to ecclesiastical matters—any detailed description of the many mosques and tombs, in and about Delhi, would be out of place; some few may, however, be briefly noticed. The great mosque or Jumma Musjid of Delhi is not far from the Fort, from which it is separated by a wide esplanade, which, being planted with fine trees, looks like a park. The mosque, with its spacious court-yard, is elevated on a lofty platform, and has a very imposing appearance. The plan is of course the usual one: the court-yard is surrounded on three sides by cloisters, there being a handsome gate-way in the centre of each; and the fourth side is occupied by the mosque itself. The cloisters and gate-ways are of red stone, but the mosque is inlaid with marble; its three domes and two lofty minarets being of white marble, the latter relieved by perpendicular bands of red stone.

The whole country for miles round the city is strewn with the ruins of mosques and tombs—some of the latter can scarcely, indeed, be called ruins; being, many of them, in a state of almost perfect preservation. The most interesting of all these architectural remains are those known as the "Kootub,"\* situated about eleven miles from Delhi.

---

\* So named from the Mahometan Emperor Kootub ud deen, who erected the Minar as a memorial of his conquest of the Hindus in the 13th century.

This group of buildings consists of a great mosque, together with several beautiful tombs, and the celebrated Minar, supposed to be the loftiest column in India. The mosque exhibits a curious incongruity in its architecture—the great arches being most unmistakeably Mahometan in style, while the colonades of the cloisters are supported on pillars which are as unmistakeably Hindoo. The carving on the great central arch is extremely beautiful; but the whole of this part of the building is in a very decayed state, and threatens a speedy fall. The Minar, which is about 250 feet high, is divided by projecting galleries into five stages, the three lower of which are fluted and of red stone, the two highest being of white marble relieved by stone bands.

The entire surface of the three lower stages is covered with carving and inscriptions, remaining as clear and sharp in outline as if cut only a year or two ago. From the top of the Minar the view is wonderful: the whole surface of the country, as far as the eye can reach, being covered with ruined mosques, &c.; and in several places are to be seen the ruins of entire towns with their fortifications. There is a traveller's bungalow in the enclosure of the Kootub, where we had tiffin, and then proceeded to explore the ruins still further on. There is a great drawback to one's pleasure in visiting these places, and that is, the tail of natives which collects and follows you about. Moreover, as soon as we approached any tomb or building of apparent antiquity, some individual would sneak into the place; so as to appear, when we entered, as the presiding genius of the edifice (although probably knowing no more about it than we did), and on the strength of this, would demand "backsheesh."

A large village has sprung up among the ruins beyond the Kootub, and there is here a tank some 150 feet by 40, I should think, and I dare say 60 feet deep to the surface of the water. At one end steps lead down to the water, but at the opposite end there is a perpendicular wall. On arriving at this place, we were amazed to see at least half of our motley escort divest themselves of the small allowance of garments which they had on, and, one after the other, jump clean off the edge into the water sixty feet below. They jumped off in a curious but not ungraceful sort of flying attitude, and when half way down suddenly brought their feet close together, and with their arms raised straight above their heads, plunged into the water like a knife, with scarcely any noise or splash. Our visit to the Kootub occupied a whole day ; but both on our way there and back, we stopped more than once to examine some of the many beautiful tombs which line the road. Most of the larger buildings are very much alike, being all built something on the same plan as the celebrated Taj Mehal at Agra. They are generally octagonal or rather square with the angles cut off. In the centre of each of the four larger sides is a lofty portal, the openings in the angles being in double tiers. The centre of the building is occupied by a circular or octagonal chamber, covered by the great dome and containing the tomb, while surrounding the central chamber, are two stories of smaller chambers. Almost every one of these buildings stands on an elevated platform at the end of a garden, which is itself enclosed and entered by a handsome gateway. The buildings of this class near Delhi are almost all of red stone inlaid with white marble : the central dome and four smaller domes over the angles being entirely of marble.

Few visitors to Delhi quit it without taking a stroll through the Cashmere Gate and its vicinity—the scene of the great struggle during the assault in 1857. The gate itself contains two arches, one for exit, the other for entrance ; and as both it and the fortifications near seem to have received no repairs since the assault, one is able to realize what a storm of cannon balls must have been launched upon it. The wonder is, considering the dilapidated state of the gate and walls, that so few marks of the bombardment are visible within the city itself. The European Cemetery is just outside the gate; and here lie those who fell in the assault, together with the victims of the atrocious massacre which took place within the city. The burial ground is on the slope of a hill, and is kept in very good order—indeed, the whole city is so neat and orderly, that it is difficult to believe that ten short years ago it was a scene of anarchy and bloodshed. I had almost forgotten to mention the Public Gardens, which are close to the Railway Station, and are very prettily laid out with abundance of flowers—which, unlike the flowers in Madras, have somewhat of that perfume we generally expect to find in flowers.

The journey from Delhi to Agra occupies some seven hours. We left at 4 p. m., and reached the Junction of the short branch line which goes to Agra at about 10. Either the road was out of order, or the carriage was, for I never experienced such a rough and noisy piece of railway travelling as this short stage from the Junction to the Agra station. I was very much reminded of my first visit to Niagara Falls in America, on which occasion every one was on the *qui vive* to obtain a first glimpse or hearing of the Falls—in the same way, on nearing Agra, all heads were out of the window, looking eagerly for the "Taj." Just before entering the station we caught a glimpse of what looked like the ghost of some great white building, very indistinctly visible in the moonlight—but it was the Taj, without doubt; and we felt that accession of dignity, which always is perceptible when, as the Yankees say, " we have seen the Elephant." The railway station at Agra is, so to speak *not* at Agra, but at the other side of the Jumna, which we crossed by a very ricketty bridge of boats. On our way to the hotel we passed the Fort, looking grand and gloomy (a perfect realization of a mediæval fortress) in the moon-light. After passing it we caught sight of the Taj, some distance down the river, looking shadowy and indistinct but beautiful, and after driving through various streets reached our hotel about midnight; went to bed and dreamt that the Jumma Musjid of Delhi and the Taj of Agra having been invited to meet the station church of Delhi, and the ditto of Agra at dinner, politely declined the acquaintance.

# CHAPTER VI.

*Agra—Fort—Taj—Akbar's tomb—Cawnpore.*

OF course the great object of attraction at Agra is the Taj ; we however deferred our visit thither until we had explored the Fort, which is far more interesting and striking than that of Delhi. Externally it realizes all one's ideas of an ancient fortress—the walls are lofty and embattled, and at each corner there is a circular tower, while the gateways are really magnificent. It retains far more of its original features than the Fort at Delhi ; and the Palace which, as at Delhi, overlooks the river, remains almost entirely in its original state. There is also here a " Pearl Mosque," but infinitely superior in every respect to the bijou Mosque at Delhi. The Pearl Mosque at Agra is of considerable dimensions, its court-yard measuring something like 200 feet each way ; and the mosque itself has five arches and five domes, instead the usual three. The mosque and the interior of the court-yard are entirely of white marble, the exterior being faced with red stone. The Palace consists of a series of beautiful white marble pavilions overlooking the Jumna ; and the walls are ornamented with precious stones inlaid in very beautiful patterns. A great deal of this decoration has been destroyed by the picking and stealing fingers of our art-loving countrymen, but enough remains to show how costly the building must have been. I observed, in places out of easy reach, tourquoises and emeralds inlaid round the windows, as well as what looked extremely like uncut rubies. My fingers itched to pick and steal after the manner of my nation, but I forbore. This wholesale plundering and destruction is now strictly forbidden. One of the "sights" of the Palace is the bath-room attached to the Zenana. It is simply a cellar, the walls and roof of which are inlaid with innumerable small pieces of looking-glass. I dare say it may have looked very brilliant when lit up, but apart from associations, it appeared to me rather tawdry, and would assuredly be universally called so if it were in the "Palace" at Sydenham, instead of the Palace at Agra. During the whole time of our visit to the Fort, we continued to steal as many glances as possible at the Taj, which was visible about three quarters of a mile down the river; and impatience to see this world-renowned building led us to quit the Fort without having seen all that we might.

I had read so much about the Taj, and had seen so many pictures and models of it, that I was almost disappointed to find it exactly what I expected. But if it did not surpass my anticipations, it certainly came up to them, at least so far as its external appearance is concerned. The gardens were more extensive than I had expected to find them, and I was not prepared for the group of buildings of which the Taj itself forms the centre. The white marble platform (300 feet square) on which the Taj stands, is itself the centre of a still larger platform, or rather paved, court-yard—bounded on its two longer sides by the garden and the river, while the two ends are occupied, each, by a large and beautiful mosque. These buildings are exactly alike, and are built of red stone with inlaid marble ornaments, and together with the Taj and the four beautiful marble minarets (each 135 feet high) at the corners of the marble platform, make up a most glorious architectural group. With the interior of the Taj, I confess I was disappointed. The central chamber, in which the tombs (which, together with the marble screen surrounding them are most beautiful,) are placed, is small in comparison with the external dimensions of the building, and its dome has no connection with the external dome. Mr. Fergusson, in his hand-book of architecture, has allowed his pen to run away with him in describing the interior of the Taj. He says, " The light is admitted through double openings filled with marble tracery of most exquisite design." The design is here faith-

fully depicted, and I think can scarcely be termed " exquisite." The system of inlaid ornament observed in the Palace is carried out to a still greater extent, and in far purer taste in the Taj. The whole of the lower parts of the walls, together with the tombs and the screen, are elaborately decorated with bloodstones, agates, cornelians, and many other precious stones, inlaid in beautiful patterns. To the very great credit of the people in general, the picking and stealing perpetrated in the Palace has not been put into practice here; and every thing remains as fresh and beautiful as on the day when it was finished. We visited the Taj under all possible circumstances—sun-shine, cloud, and moonlight: and on the latter occasion, were serenaded by some native minstrels, who played and sang sundry native airs, including, of course, " Tasa pe Tasa." Their instruments were soft and really rather sweet, very different to our Madras native instruments, and we enjoyed the music, until they horrified us by commencing, " We won't go home till morning,"—the pronunciation being something worth hearing. After this we dispensed with our serenaders, and soon after returned to the hotel. I visited the Station Church which, resembling as it does Christ Church, in Madras, formed a charming contrast to the Taj. I believe there is a decent Church in Agra, but I was not fortunate enough to find it. We devoted one day to a visit to Akbar's Tomb at Secundra, some seven miles from Agra. The building, as usual, is at one end of a large garden, enclosed by walls and entered through a large and handsome gateway. It is entirely different from most of these tombs, and is in fact a species of pyramid—consisting of, I think, five stories, which diminish in size and increase in beauty gradually, the lower being coated with plaster, the next three being of red stone, and the top one of white marble. In the centre of this, enclosed by white marble trellis-work and open to the sky, is the show-tomb, not the real tomb,—that of course being, as usual, at the base of the building. There is at Secundra a Missionary Training Institution, the existence of which I was unfortunately not aware of at the time of my visit;

and I therefore did not see anything of its arrangements. We left Agra for Lucknow late at night and reached Cawnpore, where we had to wait five or six hours, very early the following morning.

The Cawnpore station is nearly three miles from the town itself, and is the only comfortable or decent looking building that I saw in the place. The name of Cawnpore is associated with anything but pleasing recollections, and I can only say that the place itself most fully confirms any previously formed unfavourable ideas. We of course visited the Well into which the victims of the awful massacre of 1857 were thrown and still remain. The Well has been encased in dressed stone and covered in, and on the top is a marble figure of an Angel. The whole is enclosed within an octagonal screen some 20 feet high, having in one of its sides a doorway. The design is questionable second pointed (Gothic), the execution is far from good, and the material simply disgraceful. The whole ought to have been of marble, and might easily have been so; whereas it is built of the very worst stone I ever saw. The whole is discolored and in many places crumbling away; and as a memorial to our unfortunate countrymen and women is a disgrace to us. The gardens surrounding the Memorial are kept in decent order, and there are two graveyards close to the Well, in which are interred many of those who perished before the final atrocity. I also went to see the Memorial Church, and found the walls some two feet in height! and very little being done to raise them any higher. Altogether, I was utterly sickened with Cawnpore, and was very glad to cross the bridge of boats over the Ganges and take my seat in the Railway carriage which was to convey me in two hours to Lucknow.

## CHAPTER VII.

Lucknow—Kaiser Bagh—Residency—Martiniere—Church—Benares—view from the river—College—Calcutta—Cathedral.

FOR nervous individuals, who are perpetually dreading an accident all the time they are in a Railway train, I recommend a trip on the Cawnpore and Lucknow Railway. The line is straight and perfectly level, and the speed very much the same as that of a mail coach 30 years ago. It must have been a remarkably cheap line to make, seeing that there is neither bridge, cutting, nor embankment in the whole 41 miles between the two cities. With the usual perversity of Railways, this lines stops some three miles short of Lucknow, and we had a most unpleasant drive through the slums of the city before reaching our hotel. Lucknow is, apart from associations, a very imposing-looking city, and comes up to one's old ideas of Oriental splendour more nearly than any Indian city I had then seen. All its grandeur is, however, " imposing" in another sense of the word, for it is all sham, gilded wood and stucco. Close to the hotel there was a large and magnificent looking building, with a huge gilt dome, which, on going round to the back, I discovered to be only half a dome, constructed of lath and plaster, and resembling in shape one-half of a cocoanut shell. The great square of the Kaiser Bagh (the Palace) appears—until you discover the cracked plaster and rotten domes,—very splendid. The principal part of the square is occupied by flower beds, where there can fortunately be no deception. Of course the chief object of interest is the Residency, which remains, so far as the buildings are concerned, almost exactly as it was when the remnants of the European Garrison quitted it ten years ago. Every one of the buildings is more or less shattered, and although it is difficult to believe that houses built in our charming brick and plaster fashion could ever look picturesque in ruins, yet these buildings have, by means of ivy and creepers twined over them, been made to assume the appearance of venerable ruins ; and it is difficult to believe that the momentous events which have rendered them famous took place ten short years ago. One of these ruinous houses is placarded (as they all are) with the name of its owner at the time of the siege. It was Dr. Phayrer's house, where Sir Henry Lawrence died. But so completely had the aspect of the place removed the events apparently centuries back, that when a very jolly-looking gentleman was pointed out to me at a concert in Calcutta as the identical Dr. Phayrer, I looked at him with much the same feeling as I should regard Queen Elizabeth were she suddenly pointed out to me at an evening party. The Residency grounds are kept in beautiful order, and there is an artificial mound in front of the principal building, with a beautiful memorial Cross, some 40 or 50 feet high on its summit. The Church was completely demolished during the siege, and has not been restored : many of those who fell are buried in the grave-yard which surrounds it. A simple slab marks the grave of Sir Henry Lawrence, and I am sure no one can read the inscription without getting what Her Most Gracious Majesty describes as a " lump in her throat." " Here lies Henry Lawrence, who tried to do his duty,"—and at the foot, a further inscription, the exact words of which I forget, but which is a distinct commendation of the soul of the departed to the prayers of the living.

We spent a portion of Sunday in Lucknow, and attended morning service at a rather pretty Church, some 2½ miles from the Residency, on the road leading to the "Martiniere." This most extraordinary looking building was designed by General Martine as a residence for himself, and is now occupied by a branch of the Educational Establishment, which he left funds to endow. The Church is a cruciform building, with a tower and spire in the angle formed by the chancel and transept. The nave has aisles, but they are so narrow, and the piers dividing them from the nave are so massive, that they are more verandahs than aisles. The chancel is correctly fitted up with choir stalls, and the east window of three lights, is filled with good stained glass; the centre light, I think, representing the Crucifixion. There is a surpliced choir of some 12 or 14 boys, belonging to the Martiniere, and the singing was accompanied on a harmonium. The Psalms were not chanted, and perhaps it was just as well; as, judging from the manner in which the Canticles were scrambled through, to very florid Anglicans, the chanting of the Psalms in a like manner would not have been conducive to devotion or equanimity of temper. With a large school such as the Martiniere close at hand, surely a better service might be got up in this church. The boys' voices were by no means bad, but they appeared to have had no training whatever. Hymns Ancient and Modern were used.

Our visit to Lucknow was curtailed for want of time, and consequently our inspection of so interesting a place unsatisfactory; and the same remarks apply with still greater force to our hurried peep at Benares. The "Holy City" is not on the main line of railroad, and even after reaching the terminus of the branch line from Mogul Serai to Benares, you find yourself on the wrong side of the Ganges, and at least five miles from the European Cantonments. We arrived at 4 a. m. after a fatiguing night journey, and as we wished to leave again the same night, we could only snatch a couple of hours' sleep and then drove down to the river, took a boat and were rowed up before the ghauts, and river front of the city. The view of Benares from the river is I think more striking than any architectural scenery I ever saw. Rising from the water along the entire river front, which extends a good mile, there is a succession of " ghauts" or broad and lofty flights of stone stairs ; in most cases backed by an ornamental architectural screen, generally fifty or sixty feet high, and having something the appearance of the front of a mosque. Between these the steps continue to ascend and are lost among the lofty buildings which rise up in the back ground tier above tier. These buildings are of all sorts ; palaces, mosques, and Hindu temples with gilded cupolas—among the palaces, that once occupied by Nana Sahib is conspicuous, while the entire population at the time of our visit (7 a. m.,) appeared covering the broad steps leading down to the river, or bathing in the river itself. These bathers were not the only occupants of the stair and the river, for close to the edge of the waters several dead Hindus were placidly burning, while in close proximity to their living friends, sundry dead cows were washing about, and emitting anything but a pleasing odour. Indeed the whole scene although picturesque and intensely oriental, was, probably on the latter account, anything but pleasing to the nose. The streets in the city are so narrow, that we had to leave our conveyance some distance from the river and walk ; and by this means we saw far more than if we could have driven. We were too tired however to exert ourselves much, and went back to our hotel, without seeing more than the outside of the Missionary College. It is a handsome-looking building in the Tudor Gothic style, apparently correct enough in its details, but containing no one feature adapting it to the climate of India. It stands in a large compound, about half way between the native town and the hotel, which latter was close to the church. In the afternoon we went to the Botanical gardens, which are very pretty and nicely kept, though small, and at 10 p. m. started for the Railway station, where we waited till 3 a. m. for the train to start; preferring a hard bench in the waiting room to the certainty of missing the train, had we slept at the hotel.

The journey from Benares to Calcutta is most uninteresting, the country being an unbroken flat the whole way; and it is very tedious, lasting 28 hours. The dust and dirt too are nearly as bad as between Allahabad and Delhi, and we were truly thankful to arrive at 7 a. m. the following morning at the terminus, at Howrah, which, like most of the stations on this Railway, is on the wrong side of the river. We crossed the Hooghly, (which reminded me very much of the Thames, being about as wide and as dirty,) in a comfortable saloon steamer, and as there were plenty of hack carriages waiting on the other side, we soon reached our destination. I was fortunate enough, during my short stay in Calcutta, to be the guest of the Rev. W. C. Bromhead, Chaplain of St. John's, and have to thank that gentleman for my non-experience of Calcutta hotels, as well as for his very great kindness and hospitality. I confess I was grievously disappointed with the so-called "City of Palaces." It is true that the two Cyclones from which it so recently suffered have robbed it of the few trees it could once boast of, but even making allowance for that, there is little to make one comprehend how Calcutta could ever have impressed any one so much as to earn for it so high-sounding a title as it bears. Government House is a fine large building; but it is only brick and plaster; and Dalhousie (formerly called Tank) Square is rather handsome. The shops too are showy, and have large plate glass windows, like those at Home, and must be nice and hot I should think. Government House faces the "Maidan," a large open common, having on the right hand side the river and Fort William, and on the left Chowringhee row, which extends about a mile, and the view on this side is finished by S. Paul's Cathedral and the Bishop's Palace. At a distance the Cathedral looks rather well, as it has a lofty and well proportioned spire; but the illusion is soon dispelled on a nearer inspection. It is built of brick and plaster, both very bad; and the plan consists of a huge choir or chancel without aisles, but very wide, transepts not quite so wide and a sort of nave of two bays. The nave is really of three bays; but the western-most one contains a library above, and the carriage porch below, so that the vehicles actually drive into the church. The tower is at the intersection of the nave and transepts, but is not half their width, and the space is consequently blocked up by huge solid piers. The general effect, however, of this part of the building is not bad, as the tower is open to the church, and the internal height immediately under it must be at least 90 feet. The arch opening into the chancel or choir is occupied by a screen surmounted by the organ, which has a double front, like those on the screens of English Cathedrals. Indeed, the aim and object of the architect seems to have been to reproduce on a small scale, an old English Cathedral, arranged in the horrible fashion by which the congregation are all thrust into the choir, and the nave and transepts left in emptiness and desolation. The style is supposed to be Tudor Gothic, but a more pitiable parody of mediæval architecture never was seen in this or any other country. The surface of the walls both within and without, is covered with coarse plaster (not polished chunam like that used in Madras) and the whole is decorated! with pannelling on a large scale. The windows, with the exception of the East and West, are tall ungainly openings of two lights, and are filled with common glass relieved with patches of blue glass, here and there, and the roof which is of wide span, is more like that of a railway station than anything else I can compare it to. The East and West windows, having both been blown in by successive Cyclones, were at the time of my visit filled up with mats and canvas screens; but I believe they never had any mullions (the mullions of the side windows, by the way, are of wood) and the East window contained a huge painted glass picture of the Crucifixion, copied from one of West's paintings. It is to be hoped that the new window which, together with a reredos, has been ordered out from Home as a memorial to Bishop Cotton, will contain an equally satisfactory subject. Fortunately the furniture of the church is in some degree better than the building, inasmuch as it does not pretend to be what it is not. The nave and transepts are empty, with the exception of two small screened-off vestries and a few monuments. One of these is very beautiful; and consists of an Altar Tomb placed in a recess in the East wall of the North transept. The arch over the tomb is of richly carved Caen stone, and the back of the recess is occupied by a beautiful group in alabaster. I unfortunately forget the subject, and also the name of the person in whose memory the monument was erected, but the whole is undoubtedly a beautiful work of art. There is in the same transept a marble statue of Bishop Heber. The figure is kneeling, and I should imagine the likeness must be good, as the face bears a close resemblance to that in the same Bishop's monument in Madras Cathedral. The window sills in the choir are about 13 feet from the floor and the space beneath is occupied by open arches filled with venetians; this arrangement being apparently intended to promote free circulation of air. This good intention has however been almost entirely frustrated by the erection of a long row of stalls on each side rising in three tiers, like those with which we are all familiar at Home. These stalls are backed by a carved screen, and of course effectually keep off all breezes which may be blowing, from the centre of the Church, which is occupied by seats facing east. The Bishop's throne is, I think, at the east end of the stalls, on the south side, and the Governor's seat is opposite to it. Both are covered with pinnacles, and would-be gothic tracery. The choir stalls are to the east of these, and close to the Altar, which is the best feature in the Church. It stands on a white marble platform three or four steps above the floor of the choir, and was, on the occasion of my visit, vested in a handsome crimson velvet frontal and super-frontal, the former having a gold cross embroidered on it. There was a super-altar I believe, but no ornaments. These will no doubt be supplied when the new Reredos is erected. As the season was Lent, I need scarcely say that the Altar should, strictly speaking, have been vested in violet; but I doubt not that in Calcutta there are quite as many (if not more) difficulties (in the way of " anti-ritualistic" outcry) to contend against, as in Madras. The organ, as already mentioned, stands on the screen, and is a very fair instrument by Gray and Davison of London. It has three rows of keys, viz., great and choir to GG, and swell to Tenor C; together with one octave of open wood pedal diapasons to CCC. These, together with the great organ diapasons which stand, one in the East and the other in the West front, are very good, but like all Gray and Davison's organs, the mixtures are very screaming and harsh. I give, as nearly as I can remember, a list of the stops, but I know it is not quite correct.

*Great organ.* Open diapason, open diapason, stopt diapason, principal, twelfth, fifteenth, sesquialtera and cornettierce, trumpet. *Swell*, bourdon, open diapason, stopt diapason, principal, fifteenth, sesquialtera, cornopean. *Choir* stopt diapason, dulciana, principal, flute, fifteenth, keraulophon. *Pedal*, open diapason 16 feet.

The organ was very much out of order, and only one reed stop was of any use, the great organ trumpet being almost entirely dumb and perfectly useless. The organ has, however, since been entirely repaired. The case of the instrument is rather handsome, having three towers of gilt pipes in each front with a good deal of carving on the top. I attended evening service on Sunday; and perhaps the less said about the singing the better. There was a large surpliced choir, and the service was of much the same character as at Bombay as regards the music sung, but by no means as regards the manner of singing it. I must observe however that the organist, Mr. Frye, had only just arrived, and had had no time to institute the reform which, from all I heard of him, I have no doubt he has by this time effected; and indeed if he makes his choir sing as well as he plays, there will be nothing left to be desired. The Cathedral is singularly fortunate in its chaplains; and I need scarcely say in its Bishop; so that I think, on the whole, Calcutta lovers of choral service may look forward hopefully to the future. There is daily even song, (read, I think,) and a weekly celebration, at least this was the case when I was there, though I dare say there may have been changes since, and if so, they have been, we may be sure, for the better. The exterior of the Cathedral presented a most woeful spectacle. The plaster had pealed off in great flakes, leaving the brick-work exposed, and in many places, especially the buttresses, the brick-work itself had crumbled away. Each buttress was originally surmounted by a pinnacle, but the cyclones had made sad havoc among these. Scarcely one remained upright. Moreover the manner in which these ornaments were originally manufactured was brought to light; and certainly was ingenious. The pinnacles were not built of brick, but consisted simply of iron rods, like pokers, upon which the crochets and finial were moulded in plaster. In some cases the whole of the plaster had disappeared, finial and all, and the iron rod remained (no two of them quite upright, but all bowing to each other) while in others the finial remained, and looked, for all the world, exactly like the ornaments which we see represented, in prints of 1746, as gracing the summit of Temple Bar.

These pinnacles have now, I believe, been entirely removed, and it is said that the Bishop, when he first saw his Cathedral, was so horrified at the sight of these adornments; that when very shortly afterwards a design for a new Church (blossoming all over with pinnacles) was presented for his approval; his Lordship turned his head away with a shudder, and said "No, no: let us have no pinnacles, go and look at the Cathedral."

## CHAPTER VIII.

### St. John's Church—Fort Church—S. James's Church.

SINCE my visit to Calcutta, I have read Bishop Wilson's life; and it really is sad to see how his noble and self-denying exertions and efforts to raise and endow a Cathedral worthy of his Diocese have failed. As will be seen from my description, the building is a failure in every way, although it cost nearly £60,000, and the sum of £20,000 collected for endowment of a Chapter has been devoted to other objects. Perhaps Bishop Milman may be able to realise what his zealous predecessor hoped so fondly to see, and worked so diligently to bring about. The old Cathedral, St. John's, is near Dalhousie Square, and surrounded closely by houses. It is built very much in the same style as Madras Cathedral, only it is not nearly so long, and is moreover disfigured with galleries. The interior, altogether, is very like S. Martin's-in-the-Fields in Trafalgar Square. There is a small chancel, without any choir stalls however, and the East window, of three lights, is filled with very good stained glass. The pulpit and prayer-desk stand two bays west of the chancel arch and the space between is empty; but will, I believe, be eventually occupied by choir stalls. The Altar is of very fair size and the wall behind it, as well as the entire walls and roof of the Sanctuary, are painted and gilded in very good taste. The organ is in the west gallery and is a good instrument by Gray and Davison. Its

View across the transept of Calcutta Cathedral.

contents are almost exactly the same in those of the Cathedral organ, the only differences being that there is a Gamba in place of the 2nd great organ diapason, a Cremona in place of the choir Keraulophon; and there is, in addition, a Hautboy in the swell. The compass also is different, being to CC. instead of GG. I attended service at S. John's on Sunday morning, and heard a capital Sermon from the Bishop; my host, Mr. Bromehead, who is senior chaplain of the church, reading prayers. The service was not choral, but what *was* sung was done decently and in order; so far as is possible with an unsurpliced choir in a west gallery. St. Peter's Church in Fort William is, like the Cathedral, a Gothic failure—although not to such a great extent. It is copied in its main features from S. Paul's Church, in York Place, Edinburgh; but it is far smaller, and is built of brick and plaster instead of stone. The general outline, however, of the exterior, very forcibly calls to mind the features of its Edinburgh proto-type. Internally S. Peter's is decidedly ecclesiastical looking. There are no galleries, and the two eastern bays of the nave are reserved as chancel. For the benefit of those who have never seen S. Paul's, Edinburgh, I may as well mention that it and its Calcutta copy, consist merely of a nave and aisles, without the smallest rudiments of a chancel. At each corner of the nave there is an octagonal turret, and the buttresses are all surmounted by pinnacles. The style is Tudor Gothic, or "Perpendicular" and in the Edinburgh church, the windows of the aisles and clerestory are of three lights with perpendicular tracery in the heads. In the Calcutta church the side windows are of two lights only and have wooden mullions without any tracery at all. In all its internal arrangements it is very correct; perhaps more so, on the whole, than any other church in India. The Sanctuary occupies one entire bay; and the Altar, which is well raised and properly vested, is backed by a very beautiful marble and alabaster reredos. I forget the subject of the sculpture, but I think it is the institution of the Blessed Sacrament; and it is a really good work of art. The East window is of three lights and is filled with stained glass representing the Crucifixion. There is a credence table, and there are also sedilia; while the floor of the Sanctuary is laid with encaustic tiles; and the walls as well as the roof are painted and gilded. This decoration is carried over the whole roof of the church, and is on the whole effective.

The church is seated throughout with low open seats, and there are in their proper places, a handsome font and lectern. The organ, a good though small instrument by Hill, stands at the east end of the south aisle. It has two rows of keys, namely, great organ of 8 stops and swell of 6 stops, with pedal Bourdon. The choir are surpliced, and I believe sing well, though I was unable to attend a service. I was told that the Sunday evening services are fully choral, but that in the morning the psalms are not chanted; and I do not think that the Holy Communion has yet been chorally celebrated. On the whole, however, the Fort Church at Calcutta is a thing to be thankful for, especially if we compare it and its services to S. Mary's Church, Fort S. George. There is, in Fort William, and very close to S. Peter's, a Roman Church, such as would be described in the guide books as a " neat gothic structure." I had no time to examine it, and probably did not lose much. The latest addition to the churches of Calcutta is S. James's, which has been built almost entirely from subscriptions and collections got together by the energetic Chaplain, the Rev. Dr. Jarbo. The church is a large cruciform building with two Western Towers, and the original design, which looks exceedingly like one of Mr. Gilbert Scott's, seems to have been good; but, as usual in India, all is spoilt by the materials, which are brick and plaster. The aisles, which are nearly the same height as the nave, are divided into two stories, the lower serving as a species of verandah and the upper as galleries, the upper tier of arches occupying the place of a clerestory. The transepts are very deep, considering the size of the church, and the chancel, which is also very long, at least 40 feet, I should think, has an apsidal termination. The roofs are of open timber work, with a good deal of carving, but rather heavy in appearance. The walls and roof of the chancel were, at the time of my visit, in the hands of decorators, and were being profusely painted, in better taste it is to be hoped than the nave and transepts, which are painted a sort of sickly salmon colour. The chancel windows are lancets, and are to be filled with stained glass; but as the furniture was not in position, I can say nothing as to the ritual arrangements contemplated—I fear, however, that a surpliced choir is not among them. The organ stands over the west door and is a large and very handsome-looking instrument, with a 16-foot metal Diapason in front. It is the largest organ in Calcutta and contains 3 full rows of keys from CC. to G. in alt. and a pedal organ of 4 stops, one of them a 16-foot metal open diapason. The instrument was built by a Yorkshire or Lancashire maker, whose name I never heard before, and cost £800. It has some good points, but I did not much admire the quality of tone, although it is powerful enough to satisfy any one. I do not know exactly what this church cost, but judging from the fact of £800 being available for an organ, I think the sum total cannot have been short of £15,000; and it certainly reflects very great credit on Dr. Jarbo that he should have succeeded in raising such a sum. He seems to have left no fair means of obtaining money untried; indeed, as an envious friend of his assured me, he did everything but steal; the result shows what can be achieved by patience and energy. Quite late on the last evening of my stay in Calcutta, it was suddenly remembered that there was a good organ in the Presbyterian Kirk in Dalhousie Square, and off we started, hoping to get in. We managed to get the key after a great deal of trouble and stumbled up the gallery stairs in the dark, only to find the organ locked. A light was brought eventually, and we were able to see the building, which is very much in the same style as S. John's. The organ, apparently a large instrument, is in a gallery behind the pulpit, which of course occupies a central and prominent position.

# CHAPTER IX.

Bishop's College—Dum Dum—Climate of Calcutta &c.,—return to Madras.

NOT least important among the ecclesiastical institutions of Calcutta, is Bishop's College. I regret that I did not inform myself to some extent regarding statistics, such as the number of students, and other like matters; and must perforce confine myself to a slight notice of the buildings. The College is situated on the bank of the Hooghly, nearly opposite the P. & O. Company's wharf at Garden Reach; and we proceeded thither in a boat, about 5 o'clock in the afternoon. There is no proper landing place opposite the College; and our disembarkation was anything but an easy business. The buildings are of course merely brick and plaster, but the outline and general appearance call to mind some of the smaller Colleges at Cambridge. The principal entrance is under a tower with octagonal turrets at the corners, and bearing a strong resemblance to the entrance gateway of Christ College, Cambridge. On the right of this is the Chapel and on the left the Hall, with the library above it. The chapel is neatly arranged with stalls, and recalled to my mind very forcibly the appearance of the chapel of Magdalen College, Cambridge, *before its restoration*. There is a harmonium, but no organ, and the east window, of three ights, is filled with colored glass, which however bears tokens of dilapidation, having been cracked during the last cyclone.

Although the buildings generally did not suffer so much as the Cathedral from these storms, yet the exterior bears marks of their destructive effects, in the pealing off of the plaster, and other marks of injury. The grounds in which the College stands are extensive; but not by any means pretty—I suppose the cyclones are to blame for this also. I believe the affairs of the College are in a prosperous condition, and no doubt, the present Bishop will do all in his power to make it a school of true Catholic teaching. Nearly opposite the College, but a little further down the river, is the palace of the ex-king of Oude, who, among other pleasant tastes, has a fondness for wild beasts, and keeps a large stock of tigers, &c., whose nocturnal howlings must be a soothing incitement to slumber, distinctly heard as they are by the inhabitants of Bishop's College. At the time of my visit to Calcutta, the head quarters of " Puseyism" were supposed to be at Dum Dum, and here "Ritualism" was reported to ride rampant. As I had the pleasure of being acquainted with the Chaplain, the late Rev. Arthur Stone, I went out to tiffin with him one day. It was to be expected that although there were but few trees and little grass in Calcutta itself, there might be a sprinkling of both on the road to Dum Dum, but no : there was nothing but dirt, evil smells, and dust; such dust too as I never saw before. It is possible that in the Great Desert of Africa the dust storms may surpass my experiences on the road to Dum Dum, but I steadily refuse to believe that such dust is to be met with any where else. At Dum Dum itself the face of nature wore an improved aspect, and there were a few trees to be seen; although nothing like the shady roads of Madras. The Church at this station, where one regiment or more is always quartered, is a most wretched building, but Mr. Stone had done his best to make the East end, at least, decent; while his good wife had trained the school children to chant very respectably. As for "Ritualism," it would have been simply impossible in such a church and with the resources at Mr. Stone's command. He simply did his best to have things done decently and in order, and was abused and bullied in consequence. I have ever since been very glad that I was able to pay this short visit to Dum Dum, for he who was on that occasion my kind and genial host, is now at rest from all his labors, and, beyond the reach of petty persecution, is now joining in the glorious ritual of the Church triumphant as described by S. John in Revelations.

As Calcutta people are very fond of keeping up the old fiction of the "Benighted Presidency," I, as an inhabitant of the same, endeavoured to find out in what respect Bengal was more enlightened than our Southern Presidency, and so far as regards Calcutta, I was unable (except in the matter of gas) to discover wherein lay the boasted superiority of the City of Palaces. The houses in Chowringee are certainly very large, much larger than the average of Madras houses, but they are packed as closely together as the houses in Vepery; indeed closer, and Mr. A. cannot fail to see everything that goes on in Mr. B.'s house. Then there is an ever present consciousness of the existence of drains, or rather the smell which is connected with drains, as I doubt whether the latter exist to any great extent. The climate in the cool weather is pleasant enough, except that it is often chill and damp; but in the hot weather, judging from the small experience I had at the end of March, Calcutta must be a Pandemonium, such as the extreme of the hot weather in Madras can convey no idea of. I observed that the houses are larger than those in Madras; so also are the musquitoes, by many degrees; and also far more voracious. Indeed, nearly every thing in Calcutta is on a larger scale than in

Madras, even to the natives themselves; who are great not only in body but, as it appeared to me, so far as domestic servants were concerned, in laziness and impudence likewise. They will not speak English, although I am convinced that in many cases they understand it, and the result is, that their masters have to talk Hindustani exclusively when addressing them; the still further result being that our countrymen and women too in Bengal have got into the habit of interlarding their ordinary conversation with such a number of native words, that they would be in a great measure unintelligible at home. However benighted Madras may be in some respects, we at least are far ahead of Bombay or Calcutta, especially the latter, in that English is the language in which we carry on business with the natives and in which we speak to each other. A Bengal European calls his Butler a "Kansamah" (spelling doubtful), and that functionary answers "Sahib." In Madras, the Butler says "Master" and the Master says "Butler." Even the use of the word "Tiffin" is becoming obsolete in the benighted city, and we have long ago decided that it is quite as rational to call "Early tea" by its English name as by a Tamil or Hindustani one.

I attended a concert in Calcutta, and here again I felt that I was not called upon to hide my diminished head and blush for Madras. I will say this, however, that a Calcutta audience is infinitely more reasonable and more easily pleased than a Madras assembly of the same nature.

As regards matters ecclesiastical, things look very hopeful in Calcutta; but lay help is much wanted. There was at the time of my visit, no branch of the E.C.U., though both Madras and Bombay had established associations in connection with that Society some time previously. On the other hand, however, annual choral festivals have been held, with I believe considerable success, in S. Paul's Cathedral for the last four or five years ; while we are in this respect still benighted.

Our very limited visit to Calcutta soon came to a close and we embarked early on a Tuesday morning on board the P. and O. Company's steamship "Surat." The "Surat" is a noble ship of nearly 2,600 tons register, and is exceedingly comfortable. We had about 60 passengers, and as the officers were very musical, and there were both a piano and a harmonium in the saloon, our evenings were enlivened by singing and playing. The passage down the river was, as usual tedious, and we did not get to sea till Wednesday morning. The voyage was without incident or even sea sickness, and we anchored in Madras Roads on the following Saturday at 1 p.m; thus bringing our tour, and consequently my "notes" thereof to a conclusion.

www.ingramcontent.com/pod-product-compliance
Lightning Source LLC
Chambersburg PA
CBHW020857230426
43666CB00008B/1221